RELATIONSHIP THERAPY FOR COUPLES

Workbook & Guide

Emotionally Focused Therapy Activities & Guided Conversations Proven To Resolve Conflicts, Grow Stronger, More Connected & In Love Than Ever Before

SAMANTHA JONES

First Printing Edition, 2024
Printed in the United States of America
Available from Amazon.com and other retail outlet

Growing Together

As you and your partner work through the pages of this book, I hope you're finding moments of clarity, connection, and self-discovery that are truly helping you strengthen your relationship.

I understand how busy life can be, and I genuinely appreciate your time. If you could spare just a couple of minutes to share your thoughts in a review on Amazon, it would mean the world to me.

Simply scan the QR code above, and you'll be taken directly to the book review page—it's quick and easy!

Your feedback not only helps me improve this book, but it could also inspire other couples to pick it up and embark on their own journey toward deeper love and understanding. Your words might be the encouragement they need to take that first step.

Thank you so much for considering this small but meaningful way of giving back.

With gratitude,

Samantha Jones

Introduction

Every relationship is a blend of unique personalities shaped by individual traits and backgrounds. While we may be different people, if we want to experience the joy of finding peace in one another, we must learn how to create a thoughtful story out of those differences.

Like every couple, you and your partner must navigate the complexities of making a relationship work despite these differences. By now, you've likely realized how challenging that can be. It requires more than just staying in the relationship. Often, you need guidance—something to shed light on those grey areas and help you better understand the nature of your relationship.

I know this journey well. My own relationship, at one point, felt like it was strained by time and small unresolved issues that began to pile up over the years. It wasn't one big conflict that threatened to tear us apart; rather, it was the accumulation of those seemingly insignificant moments—forgotten anniversaries, unspoken disappointments, and unmet expectations—that gradually created a negative cycle. We became trapped in a routine where each minor issue compounded the next. Conversations that used to be lighthearted turned into tension-filled exchanges, and soon, we were caught in a loop of blame, frustration, and misunderstanding.

Like many couples in this situation, we found ourselves standing at a crossroads—wondering whether we should give up or fight to restore what had once been so precious. There was a sense of desperation, a fear that perhaps we wouldn't find another chance to experience this kind of connection again with someone else. In that moment of doubt, we made a decision: to work on our relationship, to actively choose to stay and rebuild.

And that decision alone brought a shift. We hadn't solved our issues overnight, but the act of committing to the relationship—to both ourselves and each other—lifted a weight. We knew that we were in it together. But the real transformation occurred when we moved the focus from ourselves and our individual needs to each other's needs.

For instance, I stopped thinking solely about how I was feeling neglected and instead began asking how my partner felt after a long day, or what stress they were carrying that might have caused them to snap earlier. Instead of waiting for my partner to initiate quality time, I took the first step—organizing a weekend getaway or just sitting beside them on the couch, quietly holding hands without words. These small, practical acts of focusing on the other person made a world of difference. Slowly, the walls of resentment that had built between us started to crumble. I could feel the shift in my partner as well. They, too, started asking how they could support me, and we began approaching our relationship as a team again.

What we realized was that the magic didn't happen from grand gestures or sudden epiphanies; it was in the everyday decision to put each other first in small ways. And with each act of consideration, the cycle of negativity reversed. There were still tough moments—those don't disappear—but now we approached them with an attitude of "How can we fix this together?" rather than "How did you hurt me?"

This book, in many ways, is an extension of that journey. It takes the Emotionally Focused Therapy (EFT) approach, offering practical, evidence-based principles to help resolve differences and strengthen emotional bonds between couples. As we move forward, you will learn about the fundamental benefits of building a secure emotional connection, the importance of understanding your relationship, and how to navigate its strengths and weaknesses to build a resilient, lasting partnership.Additionally, we will explore how to create and understand attachment, techniques to recognize and manage negative patterns, the significance of emotional accessibility, how to manage emotional triggers, and how to make lasting, effective changes in your relationships.

You'll also likely agree that any relationship—whether romantic, platonic, or professional—requires effort from all involved. Human differences shape our views and expectations. However, if you aim to do more than just coexist or tolerate your partner, you must also be prepared to embrace their differences.

Being with someone you love can feel like a reprieve from the world's problems. In reality, it doesn't mean you won't face challenges, but a good relationship serves as a beacon of hope—a reminder that good things can come and stay. While it's easy to meet someone, fall in love, and enjoy the initial charm, maintaining a relationship is far from effortless. People's reasons for this vary, but one thing universally understood is that learning and truly understanding another person is difficult. Many even consider it impossible.

However, the notion that you cannot truly know a person implies you can't fully love them either. To be loved is to be known. Reoccurring conflicts might make you feel like you don't know your partner at all, but the key to a stronger relationship lies not in viewing your partner as a stranger but in working to understand them and resolving conflicts with a mindset focused on mutual compromise.

This book is designed to help you find strength without shying away from vulnerability. It will guide you in exploring the complexities of your partner's world—someone who now holds an essential place in both your life and heart. My goal is to help reignite your passion, heal what has been broken, and help you create the love life you desire.

Even as we live in a fast-paced, ever-changing world filled with stressors—be they social, emotional, financial, or psychological—what remains unchangeable is the power of love to evoke deep feelings. From Shakespeare's time to the present day, love stories have captured the hearts of people like us, serving as reminders that, despite the chaos, it's still possible to pause, embrace what you truly want, and nurture a love that endures the tough times.

This workbook is not here to drain your soul without filling it with valuable tips and hacks that will help you love your partner more deeply. It emphasizes practical strategies for improving your relationship, focusing on building and nurturing a healthy romantic connection. It includes exercises that are tried and tested to positively change the trajectory of your love life.

As you dive into each theme, remember that you are at the center of this exploration—learning how to heal old wounds and bloom in love together. This book will encourage you to assess your daily life to see how arguments, misunderstandings, and unresolved issues may strain your relationship. Most importantly, it will help you uncover what needs to change for your relationship to flourish.

Taking a practical approach to strengthening your relationship is like hitting a "call to action" button. Instead of dwelling on what could have been, you'll begin focusing on what you can actively do to achieve the results you desire. But remember, it's perfectly okay to take things at your own pace.

The importance of moving slowly, especially when dealing with emotional topics like building a healthy relationship, cannot be overstated. Your love life has the potential to become a cornerstone of your happiness, and cultivating love takes time. Just as you would wait patiently for a seed planted in spring to bloom in its season, it's okay to nurture your relationship and trust that growth will come when the time is right.

Each chapter in this book captures a theme that may resonate differently depending on where you are in your relationship. While I cannot predict which chapter will give you the answers you seek, I am confident that one will resonate deeply enough to get you started. If you've been working on healing yourself but need guidance, alternative perspectives, or just reassurance that you're on the right track, this book will meet you where you are.

Within these pages, you'll also find practical guides to strengthen your relationship, so set aside time to engage with them. A few hours a week is all it takes. And if you feel the need for a break to reflect or practice the lessons you've learned, be kind enough to grant yourself that time away from reading.

Finally, this book offers practical tools like reflective journaling, a strengths and weaknesses inventory, communication mapping, and other methods designed to help you navigate your relationship with self-awareness, discovery, and compassion. By combining these techniques, you'll be equipped to handle conflicts, rebuild trust, and enhance intimacy in ways that bring you and your partner closer.

Typically, couples may seek therapy with a third-party mediator to facilitate difficult conversations and help resolve recurring conflicts. However, in this workbook, you and your partner are your own guides. While this presents its own set of challenges, it also offers a unique opportunity for the two of you to grow stronger together. Without the presence of an external therapist, you must be disciplined in how you approach these exercises, especially when conversations become difficult. There will be moments when things get tough, but it's crucial that both of you commit to stepping back when needed. Allow yourselves the space to pause, breathe, and revisit a difficult topic at another time.

Remember, the goal is to ensure that what happens in your "couples therapy" time—this book—stays within the context of that time. Bringing unresolved issues or sensitive conversations outside of this framework could strain your everyday interactions. While it's important to carry forward the good lessons and positive changes you make, the difficult parts of your conversations should remain within the boundaries of your dedicated work together. This structure will allow you to manage emotions in a contained, productive way. With mutual understanding and discipline, this approach can make your relationship stronger over time, even though the path won't always be easy.

The tools and strategies shared in this book are not theoretical—they are the exact methods that helped my own relationship. My partner and I still use them today to maintain our connection, just as we did in those crucial first months when we decided to work on us. They've kept our relationship as strong as it was when we first made the choice to rebuild, and I hope they serve you just as well.

If you find even one piece of advice that brings you closer or helps you see things in a new way, I'd be truly grateful if you would leave a review. Your feedback means the world to me, and even if it's just one nugget of gold that makes a difference in your relationship, sharing that can help others on the same path.

I WANT TO LEAVE
A REVIEW!
SCAN THIS QR-CODE

Thank you for trusting me to be part of your journey.

Week 1

Understanding Your Relationship

"No relationship is perfect" is the famous mantra that might get you thinking it is okay to keep pushing the hard pill of an unhealthy relationship down your throat. When a romantic relationship meant to help you through a tiring and stressful day becomes part of your frustration, running under the shade of imperfection becomes effortless.

The truth is, it does offer a type of consolation. Something within you needs to know that you are not alone and that many romantic partners are learning the water too (and maybe drowning) – a made-believe illusion that can offer you a temporary calm. But alas, you are up again, and instead of taking the next right decision, you are somewhere wondering how you can paddle this poorly structured canoe. But you don't have to live like that.

Whether in life or a relationship, you benefit significantly from comprehending a disturbing situation. This ensures that you do not make an impulse decision or rely on mere surface facts to conclude. In reality, understanding the problem is how we point out the grey areas, find answers entirely different from what society provides us, and make a resolution that serves our best interest.

It seems like your relationship is constantly on a rocky path because you've never tried to imagine a world where you finally learn to unpack the baggage of individual differences. While it may seem like forging forward offers a temporary bliss – like helping you meet the need to be in a relationship – what is certain is that no one can embark on a lifelong journey with a heavy backpack. Not only will that take away the fun of the trip, but getting to the destination may become impossible, too.

For once, I need you to embrace courage and give your relationship a fresh and excellent chance. Yes, I understand that the faithful and audacious part of you decided to give love a chance (or another chance) but do not let this fact blindside you from building a relationship that aligns with your interest. What is worth doing is worth doing well, and if any part of you believes in any part of that, then it is time to understand that it applies to everything, including your love life.

I get that it is tiring to think a relationship founded on mutual love and interest is becoming a little too hard to maintain, but learning to understand and manage every trait that characterizes your relationship requires you to explore the good and bad sides of things. Then, perhaps, as you do that, you will also learn that resolving your differences has always been possible.

Time and life ordeals will sufficiently test your relationship, but those moments will also allow you to assess and reassess your relationship. It won't matter whether you classify your relationship as rocky or flourishing; in reality, being in love is another way to acknowledge the need to learn daily. If you are trying to make this work, then not ignoring the details is one of the things you must do.

Understanding the Dynamics of Relationship

If you were to imagine what an ideal relationship will look or feel like, I'm sure your answer won't be far from establishing a type of relationship where both partners feel respected, valued, cherished, and allowed to flourish. While this answer is not wrong, what often determines the feature of your relationship is the dynamic of your relationship. In other words, where exactly does your relationship belong despite its ever-changing nature?

To answer this question, you've got to understand that there are several relationship dynamics. Even better, you must note that despite the differences in features of relationships, relationship dynamics are not mutually exclusive. What turns into years of relationship for most couples didn't necessarily start as one. For some, platonic relationships bloomed into healthy romantic relationships, and for others, what began as a casual relationship metamorphosed into an intense emotional connection. Over time, they learned to nurture it. I get that nurturing takes strength, and the fact that you married your best friend doesn't mean your relationship will be free of ups and downs, but it does mean that the road that led you here wasn't necessarily a clearcut one.

Understanding the relationship dynamics that brought your relationship this far also helps you appreciate how far you've come and how many differences you've learned to resolve. In doing this, you are bound to understand that constructing a because by doing that, you can identify where you are standing with your partner, identify the factors obstructing your way to a blissful relationship, and determine what needs to be done to navigate these good and bad times.

To find an answer, you need to self-assess your relationship.

I get that you think you are the worst judge of your relationship. We have all lived under the idea that it is impossible for partners to analyze their relationship and identify the loopholes therein. Somehow, we were made to believe that a stranger can do that better. But the truth is, you will always understand your relationship better because relationships are a matter of emotions, and you can only tell what that is like. Only you can experience and express how good someone makes you feel. Does it not sound like you are doing a terrible job if you leave another person to judge your relationship and even name it for you?

It may seem like you won't find the answer, but have you ever taken a holistic look at things instead of relying on a third-party idea of what is?

And if your answer is No, then it is time to stop doing that. You need to assess your relationship and uncover the strengths and weaknesses that characterize it.

At this stage, it is possible to wonder what you are looking for in your relationship or what to focus on.

Relationship dynamic refers to the complex interplay of emotions and patterns that often determine what truly exists between two partners. So, let's say you are trying to understand the dynamics of your relationship; learning about each other's emotions is a great way to start. By doing this, you will realize that you can learn more about your relationship because how you feel about someone determines how you treat them, and how someone thinks about you determines how they treat you, too.

Since healthy relationships often feature trust, open communication, respect, and fairness, finding out about the presence of this factor can even help you understand the current situation and the reasons for your struggle. Understanding the dynamics of a relationship reflects the urge to see how these factors characterize the relationship.

A relationship can't survive without trust, but one thing about trust is you must earn it. It is not a delicious apology offered in a fancy restaurant to keep you waiting; even that is earned if you think about it. In reality, there must be instances that prove to your partner that they can trust you and that you can do the same. Trust is founded on open communication because before you learn to trust someone, there must have been instances of essential communication (question and answer) that made you finally feel you can do that.

Respect and fairness are the other parts of a healthy relationship. Where respect is lacking, a partner may struggle with low self-esteem because the main person who ought to see them as worthy doesn't. Fair treatment does not entirely obliterate the place of power dynamics in your relationship.

While the power dynamic of a relationship must be observed and understood, what is essential is that each partner must feel a sense of equality and fairness for the relationship to survive. Hence, while trust and open communication are at the foundation of a relationship, trust and fair treatment maintain the relationship.

To determine your relationship dynamic through self-assessment, you must be able to provide honest answers to questions like

- *What does effective and honest communication mean to me?*
- *Do I find my partner trustworthy, and do I think they trust me too?*
- *What is the power dynamic in my relationship?*
- *How does the power dynamic change from one person to another*
- *Can I say that I and my partner feel safe in the presence of each other, and can I trust my partner to treat me reasonably even in situations where they get to make decisions that affect the both of us? Can they also trust me the same way?*
- *What are the boundaries set in our relationship, and how well has my partner respected my boundaries and vice versa?*

Getting answers to each question may require that you play and replay scenarios in your head to ensure that your answers truly represent the truth of your relationship. The answers you get here will shed the ultimate light on building a stronger relationship.

———

Identifying Strengths and Weaknesses

A resilient relationship is not perfect; instead, it is a type that has been tested with strengths and weaknesses but survives despite the bad times. While what is considered strength in your and your partner's traits makes you enjoy the relationship more, weakness can be a gigantic pain in the ass.

You may want to ask, what do I do with our weaknesses?

But to get an answer, you must ensure that you are not fixating only on the bad sides of things. Yes, a perfect relationship may be farfetched because every relationship is a woven thread of two individuals' strengths and weaknesses. Still, with a clear and deep understanding of each other's strengths and weaknesses, you can form the foundation of a lasting partnership.

Even a tumultuous relationship can feel nostalgic, and a well-established one can make you feel like you are at a dead-end. No matter the dynamics of your relationship, feeling loved or ignored is a question of when. However, any relationship can benefit significantly from an honest exploration of what makes the relationship feel like home and the things that sometimes appear capable of driving you apart.

When you are set to identify these factors in your relationship, it is vital to understand that the purpose of this exercise is not to find your partner's flaws or blame them; instead, it helps you know what needs to change for your relationship to feel good, resolve ongoing tension, and build a more. Each individual must do an honest task here, identifying and stating their strengths and weaknesses.

At this point, it becomes clear that you are embarking on a journey of self-discovery because even if it is not the first time, you will still stumble on the fact you never paid attention to. For instance, it is easy to ignore our strengths while focusing on our weaknesses, and when a relationship becomes comfortable, we tend to do the same for our partner. Things they do that make us feel good become regular, unappreciated efforts. This is why exploring this aspect of your relationship is vital to continual growth, respect, and mutual love. The wave of the bad things can blindside you from seeing the good ones, but your partner on the other side wants to be appreciated for the effort they put into making you feel special.

Cultivating the habit of identifying strengths and weaknesses and checking to see how you've managed them so far is also an excellent way to understand the dynamics of strengths and weaknesses. Nothing is entirely black and white in life or a relationship; hence, what was considered a source of strength in one situation can become one's weakness in another. For instance, if a partner had learned to perfect the art of compromising, this may be considered a source of strength because a relationship revolves around the wants of two different people, and sometimes, they don't want the same thing - here being able to compromise will be a good strength, but it can be a weakness too if a partner starts to exploit this trait.

On this journey, you will also benefit from self-awareness. Knowing that you are not perfect and being ready to explore options to improve your relationship with your partners helps build a deeper connection.

In the face of inevitable storms, strengths – such as shared values, communication, respect, honest communication, and emotional connection – form the bedrock of a flourishing love life. On the other hand, weaknesses manifest in ongoing tension and unresolved emotional wounds. Often, these are things that create an open crack in your relationship and, when left unresolved, can form a giant crack and threaten your relationship. Thus, you both must understand that this is not an aspect of your relationship that can wait because you do not want your partner to deal with the consequences of the weakness alone.

I also do not think weaknesses are the bad guys because we are all imperfect people. A bad listener is not just a bad listener; when considered in a romantic relationship, this flaw becomes a weakness that can truncate open communication and make a partner feel less valued. Yet, despite the lousy side of weaknesses, there is potential for growth and transformation in them. Acknowledging these areas of struggle can pave the way for a meaningful conversation, turning weaknesses into newfound strengths and healing from the pain and emotional wounds suffered before exploration.

It is also vital to keep at the back of your mind that this is beyond a mere surface-level conversation. Instead, it is one dedicated to ensuring that you highlight the area of both of your lives that requires personal and mutual improvement for things to get better. As you explore this path, showing vulnerability and being prepared to answer tough questions are two things that will tune this into a fruitful experience.

Common Triggers in Relationships

Triggers in a relationship occur when a situation evokes memories of past experiences. As much as we may want to leave the past behind, our brains excel at storing emotional memories. When similar patterns or events arise, it's common to react based on these old memories, often unconsciously.

Emotional triggers can vary greatly from one couple to another, often rooted in past experiences, unmet needs, or long-held expectations. While research has identified many of these factors, only you can pinpoint the exact triggers that resonate most deeply with your own experiences. The complexity of human individuality means that each person's emotional triggers can be vastly different, even within the same relationship.

PERCEPTION PARTNER 1	PERCEPTION PARTNER 2

Here are some common triggers that can surface in relationships, along with examples of how they manifest:

Insecurity: Insecurity often arises when one partner feels unsure about their place in the relationship. This can be triggered by small actions, such as a partner being less affectionate than usual, or more significant ones, like a partner's growing friendship with someone else. For example, if you've experienced betrayal in the past, seeing your partner being overly friendly with a colleague might trigger feelings of jealousy, leading to heightened anxiety or anger.

Abandonment: The fear of abandonment is a deeply rooted emotional trigger for many people, especially those who have experienced loss or neglect in childhood. This fear can be triggered when a partner appears emotionally unavailable or physically distant. For instance, if your partner comes home late from work without explanation, it might trigger feelings of being forgotten or neglected, leading you to react defensively or withdraw emotionally.

Rejection: Feeling rejected, whether emotionally or physically, can be a painful trigger. This can occur when a partner dismisses your thoughts or opinions, or when physical intimacy is consistently avoided. For example, if your partner casually disregards your idea during a conversation, it might remind you of past experiences where you felt unheard or unimportant, leading to frustration or shutting down.

Criticism: For some, criticism—even when it's constructive—can be a powerful trigger. If you grew up in an environment where you were frequently criticized, a small critique from your partner might feel like an attack, causing defensiveness or resentment. For example, if your partner points out a small mistake, it might trigger a sense of inadequacy, making you feel like you're constantly failing in the relationship.

Control: Control triggers can surface when one partner feels their autonomy is being restricted or undermined. If you've had experiences where you felt powerless or dominated, situations where your partner tries to make decisions for you—even with good intentions—can evoke a strong emotional reaction. For instance, if your partner makes a decision about your weekend plans without consulting you, it might trigger feelings of losing control, leading to frustration or rebellion.

Comparisons: Being compared to others—whether ex-partners, friends, or even family members—can stir feelings of inadequacy. If you've ever been compared negatively to someone else, even a small remark from your partner about someone else's success or behavior can trigger feelings of inferiority. For example, if your partner mentions how someone they know is "really driven" in their career, you might internalize it as a critique of your own efforts, leading to self-doubt or resentment.

Neglect: Emotional neglect triggers often arise when one partner feels ignored or unappreciated. This can be triggered when a partner seems too absorbed in work, hobbies, or other activities to give the relationship proper attention. For instance, if your partner is constantly checking their phone during your conversations, it might remind you of past moments when you felt overlooked, sparking feelings of sadness or frustration.

Lack of Affection: Physical or emotional affection is crucial in a relationship, and its absence can be deeply triggering. If affection is withdrawn, it may remind someone of times in their life when love and care were absent, leading to feelings of isolation. For example, if your partner stops being physically affectionate for a period of time, it might trigger feelings of not being wanted, resulting in emotional withdrawal or confrontation.

Financial Stress: Money is often a sensitive issue in relationships, and financial stress can trigger feelings of inadequacy or fear. If one partner grew up in a financially unstable household, even minor discussions about budgeting or spending can evoke anxiety. For instance, if your partner questions your spending habits, it might remind you of a time when financial strain caused tension, triggering defensiveness or guilt.

Unmet Expectations: When personal or relationship expectations aren't met, it can create a sense of disappointment or frustration. If you had envisioned certain milestones, such as marriage or buying a home, but your partner doesn't share those goals, it can trigger feelings of resentment or doubt about the relationship's future. For example, if your partner doesn't seem interested in discussing long-term plans, it might stir up anxiety about whether you're both on the same path.

———

Techniques for Identifying Patterns

If you must improve your relationship, conscious and dedicated effort is required. First, you must know that your relationship is made up of patterns - some you want to change, some you want to keep – then you must identify these patterns and understand their impacts. Deciding on the following line of action relies entirely on gaining a more profound understanding of your relationship. It is how you identify the factors that help you grow stronger in love, and the ones that drag you behind result in continual conflicts and reoccurring disappointments.

Reflective Journaling

Journaling means documenting everything, including the words unexpressed. In it, you write a lot about your choices, how situations and treatments made you feel, and how you develop responses to them. Documenting also means that you get to capture genuine emotions in every moment and even feel them again.

First, get a journal and tag it as "Reflective Journal for Self-Awareness and Recognition of Patterns." After this, introduce the process to your partner and dedicate time at the end of the day to writing down everything that happened in your relationship.

With this, you will not only learn about the good times but also learn more about the factors that often result in conflict. These factors eventually become indispensable in building a resilient and loving relationship.

Communication Mapping

Yes, it is true that you understand people better with time and reach a point where even their silence means something; however, you do not need to navigate an ambiguous relationship or put someone in one if you master effective communication.

A communication map helps you highlight how you communicate with your partner effectively. This prevents the idea of made-up excuses on the part of each partner and often mirrors the relationship's growth sincerely.

Create a visual map that tracks the flow of communication between you and your partner. Take notes of important things like how communication is initiated by both parties, who initiates communication often, how communication progresses between you and your partner, and how conflict or differences discussed are resolved.

Trigger Identification

Earlier, we discussed common triggers in relationships, but it's important to remember that not every possible emotional trigger can be captured. While some of the examples mentioned may resonate with you, there may be unique triggers that you and your partner need to identify and address.

For a relationship to truly flourish, both partners must work toward healing from past pain. This requires paying close attention to situations that trigger specific emotional reactions in yourself and your partner. It's about understanding what sparks certain emotional responses, whether they be anger, sadness, frustration, or anxiety.

To help with this process, your journal becomes a powerful tool. Rather than documenting every minor issue repeatedly, use your journal to translate each significant moment—how it made you feel, what emotions surfaced, and how you reacted. It's not just about recording events; it's about reflecting on the emotional impact of those moments and understanding the patterns behind your reactions.

To guide you in this process, you can refer to the list of journaling prompts provided.

Journaling Prompts for Trigger Identification

1. **Reflection on Emotional Reactions:**

   - *Think back to a recent conflict or emotionally charged moment with your partner. What was the situation, and how did you feel? Write down the emotions that surfaced.*
   - *What was it about this situation that caused you to react so strongly? Can you connect it to any past experiences, fears, or insecurities?*
   - *Was there a particular word, tone, or action from your partner that heightened your emotional response? How did you respond in return?*

2. **Connecting the Present to the Past:**

   - *Is there a pattern in how you've reacted to similar situations before, either in this relationship or in previous ones? Describe any similarities.*
   - *How might past experiences (childhood, family dynamics, previous relationships) influence your emotional triggers in the present? Can you identify any recurring themes?*
   - *What unresolved emotions from your past might be amplifying your current reactions? How do these past wounds show up in your relationship now?*

3. **Physical & Emotional Cues:**

   - *When you experience a trigger, what physical sensations arise in your body (e.g., tightness in the chest, clenching fists, racing heart)? Write down your physical responses.*
   - *How do you typically express your emotions during triggering moments? Do you withdraw, become defensive, raise your voice, or shut down? Reflect on your behavior.*
   - *What thoughts typically run through your mind when you're triggered? Do you have any repeating narratives or beliefs (e.g., "I'm not enough," "They don't care") that come up?*

4. **Your Partner's Triggers:**

   - *Are there situations where you notice your partner being triggered? How do you observe their emotional responses?*
   - *How do you typically respond to your partner when they're triggered? Do you feel more empathetic, frustrated, or helpless in these moments?*
   - *In what ways can you both create a safer space to talk about each other's emotional triggers without judgment or defensiveness?*

5. **Coping with Triggers:**

- *What coping mechanisms do you use when you feel triggered (e.g., shutting down, lashing out, avoiding the issue)? How do these strategies help or hinder the situation?*
- *Have you found any healthy ways to manage your emotional triggers in the past? What worked, and what didn't? Reflect on any growth or insights you've gained so far.*
- *What can you do differently next time a similar situation arises? List specific actions or strategies you can use to manage your emotions and communicate more effectively with your partner.*

6. **Healing and Moving Forward:**

- *Are there any unresolved emotional wounds or fears that you need to address? Write down any past issues or traumas you believe still affect you.*
- *What steps can you take to begin healing these wounds? Who or what can support you in this process (e.g., your partner, therapy, self-care practices)?*
- *How can you and your partner work together to minimize triggering situations in your relationship? Write down any changes you'd like to see, and how you can both contribute to those changes.*

7. **Reframing Your Reaction:**

- *After reflecting on the last triggering moment, ask yourself, "Could I have reacted differently?" Write down alternative ways you could have responded that might have de-escalated the situation.*
- *What could your partner have done differently to avoid triggering you, and how can you kindly communicate this to them?*
- *If you had to describe the situation from a place of empathy for both yourself and your partner, how would you do it? How does reframing the situation change your understanding of what happened?*

8. **Creating Safety and Trust:**

- *What do you need from your partner in moments of emotional distress or when you feel triggered? How can you communicate these needs clearly?*
- *What can you do to make your partner feel emotionally safe, especially when they experience triggers? Reflect on ways to offer reassurance and support during tough times.*
- *How can both of you ensure that triggering moments don't lead to resentment or disconnection? Write down steps for how to maintain trust and closeness even after conflict.*

Strengths and Weaknesses Inventory

A strengths and weaknesses inventory is like keeping a record of things. Consider it a regular inventory you will need in any organization if managing goods, sales, and profit is essential. A strengths and weaknesses inventory is just like a regular inventory; however, instead of keeping a record of goods, you are documenting factors and moments highlighting strengths and weaknesses in your relationship.

The first step is to work on what you perceive as strengths or weaknesses in your individual space. Your reflective journal will be a lucky charm here as it allows you to identify how you felt in different situations by simply rereading your journal. Each partner should take some time to complete the list provided in their journal first.

Once that is done, create a time for an honest conversation between you and your partner. Take a turn to discuss the good things you've done for each other and what you wish the other person could improve. Do this without discussing how to improve or placing blame on anyone. Fill the table together.

COMMUNICATION			
STRENGTHS	WEAKNESSES	IMPACT	ACTION PLAN

CONFLICT RESOLUTION			
STRENGTHS	WEAKNESSES	IMPACT	ACTION PLAN

EMOTIONAL SUPPORT

STRENGTHS	WEAKNESSES	IMPACT	ACTION PLAN

TRUST

STRENGTHS	WEAKNESSES	IMPACT	ACTION PLAN

EMOTIONAL INTIMACY

STRENGTHS	WEAKNESSES	IMPACT	ACTION PLAN

PHYSICAL INTIMACY

STRENGTHS	WEAKNESSES	IMPACT	ACTION PLAN

FAMILY PRESENCE			
STRENGTHS	WEAKNESSES	IMPACT	ACTION PLAN

SHARED VALUES & GOALS			
STRENGTHS	WEAKNESSES	IMPACT	ACTION PLAN

COMPROMISE & FLEXIBILITY			
STRENGTHS	WEAKNESSES	IMPACT	ACTION PLAN

VULNERABILITY			
STRENGTHS	WEAKNESSES	IMPACT	ACTION PLAN

Week 2

Building a Strong Foundation

If you were to look back at all the conflicts you've resolved with your partner and how your differences have unfolded each time you made choices, you would wonder how you came this far, learned to make mutual compromises, and forged forward despite the odds.

The general ideology that applies to almost everything is that you cannot put something on nothing with the expectation that it will stand. It further captures the fact that for every human relationship, a solid foundation is a crux. In your relationship, the level of understanding, change in dynamics, love, and support you get from your partner and offer them relies extensively on the strength of the relationship foundation. But the good part is that you can build this foundation over time and improve it without breaking it down.

For instance, starting as a partner requires some connection. For some, a simple glance is all it takes to fall in love with each other, but for others, passionate love is built over time. Whichever the case, you can agree with me that irrespective of what brought you two together, that you and your partner are making an effort to make things work better, which implies that the love that got you started was enough.

That love is enough should not cause your head to spin because, contrary to the general notion that several things make a relationship work better, being in love with someone is what makes your love life beautiful. I once heard someone make this comment: "I married the woman I know I would easily let go of almost all the unforgivable things for" and that stuck with me for a long time. You might have also realized that when you are with someone you care about, forgiveness and care aren't for them alone because those moments give you a feel of what it means to love someone. You watch hard decisions become the simplest things to do because, within you, the destination has always been known – to be with your person.

Taking the path towards that destination is often not clear, though. Sometimes, things may get complicated, and all you will have to rely on is how solid your foundation is. Building a solid foundation is what you do in the good and bad times. When love makes you feel like the problem of the world has disappeared, spending time with your partner, enhancing your connection, and expressing your love in the language they understand is how to grow your passion. Also, when things get a little too tough, and you wonder how to navigate life and your relationship, expressing your feelings honestly, seeking their opinions on how to improve any aspect of your life, and learning to forgive them helps solidify your relationship even more.

A solid foundation strengthens a relationship, but it's not just about how things began. It's about how you grow together over time. Building the life you want as a couple will inevitably test your love, sometimes making you question whether this is truly the life you envisioned. However, meaningful life choices aren't made impulsively. So, instead of falling into the trap of blaming one another when things get tough, it's essential to refocus on what truly matters.

In the early days of a relationship, everything feels fresh and exciting—trust, communication, respect, and emotional support seem effortless as you and your partner enjoy the honeymoon phase. But as time passes, and life's complexities start to build, it becomes all too easy to lose sight of those foundational pillars. Amidst the daily grind of work, bills, family, and responsibilities, even the strongest relationships may face moments when trust falters, communication fades, and emotional support feels distant.

The truth is, a solid foundation doesn't sustain itself. It requires constant nurturing. Take trust, for instance. It can easily be taken for granted. Those small promises you make to each other early on might not seem as significant as the years go by. But if you stop consciously reinforcing that trust, doubts and insecurities can creep in—even if no one has done anything overtly wrong. Trust isn't built on grand gestures; it's rooted in the everyday moments when you show up for each other, listen without judgment, and keep your word.

Communication can often be the first thing to slip in long-term relationships. What once felt like deep, meaningful conversations can gradually morph into quick exchanges about logistics—who's picking up the kids, what's for dinner, or when the bills are due. The love might still be there, but the depth of your conversations can become shallow, leaving little space for real connection. Yet, it's precisely those deeper conversations that help you stay attuned to each other's evolving needs and desires. It takes intentional effort to ensure you're not just talking at each other but with each other, truly hearing what's said and what's left unspoken.

Respect, too, can slowly erode as familiarity grows. Over time, you may find yourselves interrupting each other, dismissing feelings, or taking each other's contributions for granted. It's important to remember that respect isn't about agreeing on everything—it's about recognizing the value of your partner's perspective, even when it differs from your own. Respect means offering kindness and appreciation, even in moments of disagreement.

Emotional support is perhaps one of the most challenging things to sustain in the long run. When life feels overwhelming, it's easy to focus on your own struggles and forget to be there for your partner. You might even assume they should instinctively "know" what you need without asking. But emotional support doesn't just happen; it's built with intention. It's about checking in with your partner, offering a listening ear, and creating a space where both of you feel safe to be vulnerable. Sometimes, it's simply being present without the need to fix anything—just reminding each other that you're not alone in facing life's challenges.

In long-term relationships, these foundational elements—trust, communication, respect, and emotional support—can gradually slip through the cracks if you're not paying attention. That's why it's so important for both partners to continue working on them, together. When you invest in these core pillars, the foundation you've built will become strong enough to weather any storm, no matter how long you've been together.

This workbook is designed to help you do exactly that—work on building a strong foundation for your relationship and beyond. Through each exercise and reflection, you'll find practical steps to reinforce the trust, communication, respect, and emotional support in your relationship. By engaging with the tools provided here, you and your partner will have the opportunity to deepen your connection and create a partnership that not only survives but thrives.

Romantic relationships are a core part of our lives because we all naturally crave that special person to share life with. I want you to build a relationship that brings you joy and comfort, not heartache. Let go of the days when love made your heart ache, and embrace the moments when love becomes the beautiful force that helps you navigate even the hardest parts of life. That's what a solid foundation offers—it gives you the courage to keep growing, to keep being yourself, and to explore the possibilities you once thought unreachable.

A strong relationship provides clarity and certainty about what truly matters. It keeps you connected, helps you rebuild the bridge after an argument, and deepens your understanding of each other. A solid foundation simplifies the process of navigating your love life. As you work to strengthen it, you'll discover more about what works for both of you and what you truly want to achieve together.

Attachment Theory

The first step in building a strong relationship foundation is understanding where each partner comes from—emotionally and psychologically. How we bond and connect with our partner is deeply influenced by the attachment patterns we developed early in life. These patterns often shape the way we navigate emotional closeness, trust, and conflict in our adult relationships.

When things go wrong in a relationship, the instinct is often to question what you might have done wrong. If your partner becomes distant or communication breaks down, it's easy to blame yourself or wonder if you've caused the disconnect. However, relationships are influenced by much deeper, often invisible forces. Early psychological factors—like attachment styles—play a significant role in how we respond to intimacy, tension, and emotional needs. These attachment styles leave lasting imprints on how we approach and experience love, affecting not only how we interact with our partner but also how we interpret their behaviors.

John Bowlby, a prominent British psychologist, described attachment as a lasting bond between individuals. His research gave today's relationship experts a valuable framework for understanding how our early experiences with caregivers influence how we manage and navigate adult relationships. By examining the connection between attachment styles and emotional bonding, you can begin to see your relationship in a new light. This awareness won't necessarily turn you into a relationship expert, but it will offer you a fresh perspective when trying to find answers. You'll learn to search differently, with greater insight into the patterns that affect both you and your partner.

Emotional bonds, which are deeply rooted in our early development, are at the core of these attachment styles. From the moment we are born, emotional connections form for two fundamental reasons: safety and connection. Infants rely on their caregivers—often their mothers—not only for physical nourishment but also for emotional comfort and security. This emotional bond gives a child a sense of stability and safety, which sets the stage for how they will experience and express attachment throughout their lives.

The way an infant responds to and connects with their caregiver is shaped by the emotional environment in which they are raised. Caregivers, consciously or not, pass on their own emotional states, reactions, and behaviors to their children. If a caregiver is emotionally stable, the child will often form secure attachments. On the other hand, emotional instability or unpredictability can lead to more complicated attachment patterns, influencing how the child perceives emotional connection and support in their adult relationships. These early attachment experiences create emotional blueprints, shaping how we bond and interact in romantic relationships later in life.

Attachment Styles and Their Effects on Relationships

The innate drive of infants to form attachment combined with the availability of the attachment figure determines the type of attachment style formed by each individual. This often reflects how we measure and manage emotional connection in our adult lives. However, aside from knowing the existence of these emotional bonds, you also need to see how the type of emotional connection formed by you and your partner affects your current relationship.

While Bowlby developed the attachment theory, Mary Ainsworth took it further by helping us understand attachment styles. In her work, Ainsworth made a groundbreaking revelation about what she termed a "strange situation" by revealing the profound impacts of attachment on infants' behavior. In her research, 12-18-month-old children were observed as they responded after being separated and reunited with their mothers. The disparity in the infants' reactions led her to discern attachment styles. However, Ainsworth identified only three styles of attachment: Secure attachment, Anxious, and Avoidant. After her, Main and Solomon discovered another type of attachment called Disorganized attachment.

Secure Attachment: Infants in this category feel confident about their mother's ability to meet their needs because their mothers are also in an emotionally stable environment. Hence, they showed notable distress in the absence of their mothers and were easily comforted upon reunion.

Children who exhibit secure attachment during the research are expected to grow into adults who can build stable and healthy relationships with trust, emotional stability, and effective communication as key ingredients.

Anxious Attachment: Infants with this style of attachment doubt their caregivers' commitment due to the level of instability experienced by the mother; hence, they show heightened distress when their caregivers are not around and are also not easily comforted upon reunion. They may also develop preventive mechanisms by becoming clingy and overly dependent.

This attachment style impacts these kids' lives as they navigate into adulthood and form relationships. Kids in this category may struggle to trust their partners and require constant reassurance.

Avoidant Attachment: Infants in this category show little distress in the absence of their caregiver. Also, they ignore their caregivers upon reunion and show a notable level of self-sufficiency instead of dependency.

Infants who exhibit this type of attachment style might experience a high level of emotional closeness and independence, which may lead them to struggle with intimacy and emotional connection in adult relationships.

Disorganized Attachment: Infants with disorganized-insecure attachment were unable to deal with the absence of their mother consistently; hence, they somehow choose between being distressed or simply ignoring the fact that their caregiver is absent. They are also not necessarily excited upon reunion.

This is a style that may stem from fear or trauma. Kids in this category often grow into adults who struggle to establish stable relationships. Instead, they are frequently anxious and may become protective of their feelings.

Once you've taken the test and identified your attachment style (and that of your partner), it's important to remember that you're not confined to a single category forever. People may also exhibit a mix of two styles depending on the situation or partner. The key is to work consciously on your relationship, recognizing patterns and making adjustments to improve your emotional connection. Here are some practical steps to help:

For Those with Secure Attachment: Continue nurturing the trust and emotional connection in your relationship. Secure individuals can sometimes take the stability of their relationship for granted. Make time for meaningful communication, express appreciation for your partner, and keep reinforcing your bond through shared experiences and emotional support.

For Those with Insecure (Anxious) Attachment: Recognize when your need for reassurance might be causing strain in your relationship. Practice self-soothing techniques and communicate openly with your partner about your feelings without relying on them to constantly alleviate your fears. Learning to build self-confidence can reduce your dependency on external validation.

For Those with Avoidant Attachment: If you find yourself pulling away when things get too intimate, reflect on why that is. Intimacy doesn't equate to losing independence. Challenge yourself to be more emotionally available, share your feelings with your partner, and allow vulnerability to deepen your connection.

For Those with Disorganized Attachment: It's important to seek professional help if you feel past trauma is significantly impacting your ability to form stable relationships. While self-awareness is the first step, working through these attachment issues in therapy can help you establish healthier patterns and relationships moving forward.

It's common for partners to have different attachment styles, which can sometimes lead to misunderstandings and friction in the relationship. However, these differences don't have to become barriers; with effort and understanding, they can become opportunities for growth. Here are some practical ways to manage mixed attachment styles in a relationship:

Secure and Anxious Attachment

- For the secure partner: Be aware that your partner with an anxious attachment style may need more reassurance than you do. Offer them consistent emotional support, regular affirmations, and clarity in your communication. This will help them feel grounded and secure in the relationship.

- For the anxious partner: Understand that your secure partner may not need as much reassurance as you, and that doesn't mean they love you any less. Practice mindfulness and self-soothing techniques when you feel anxious, and remind yourself that your partner's consistent behavior is a sign of stability.

- Together: Regular check-ins and open conversations about how each of you is feeling can help. The secure partner can serve as an anchor, helping the anxious partner feel safe, while the anxious partner can learn to manage their fears without overwhelming the relationship.

Secure and Avoidant Attachment

- For the secure partner: Understand that your avoidant partner values independence and space, and it's not a reflection of their love for you. Be patient and give them the room they need, while gently encouraging more open emotional expression.

- For the avoidant partner: Your secure partner is likely comfortable with intimacy, so try to open up a bit more about your feelings. While it might feel uncomfortable at first, sharing even small emotional details can help build trust and connection. Balance your need for independence with moments of closeness.

- Together: Establish a balance where the secure partner offers emotional availability, while the avoidant partner learns to engage emotionally in a way that feels safe. Discuss boundaries openly to ensure both partners feel respected and comfortable.

Secure and Disorganized Attachment

- For the secure partner: Recognize that your partner with a disorganized attachment style may be dealing with unresolved trauma or fear of intimacy. Offer consistent reassurance and a safe emotional space, but be prepared for moments when they may pull away or act inconsistently.

- For the disorganized partner: Try to communicate your fears and anxieties, even when it feels difficult. Your secure partner is likely stable and will not abandon you. Therapy can be helpful in working through your attachment-related trauma, but in the meantime, work on trusting that your partner's emotional stability is genuine.

- Together: Therapy or counseling can be incredibly helpful for this pairing. It can provide the disorganized partner with tools to manage their emotional responses while helping the secure partner support them in a healthy way. Set a pace that feels comfortable for both partners when it comes to emotional closeness.

Anxious and Avoidant Attachment

- For the anxious partner: Your avoidant partner may not express affection in the way you need, and this can trigger your fears. Try to be mindful of your need for constant reassurance, and practice self-soothing techniques. Let your avoidant partner have space without assuming the worst.

- For the avoidant partner: Your anxious partner may need more emotional closeness than you're comfortable with. Work on slowly opening up more and being emotionally present when needed. Instead of retreating, try communicating when you need space, so they don't feel rejected.

- Together: This is a common yet challenging pairing, as one partner craves closeness while the other desires space. Communication is key. The anxious partner can learn to give space without feeling abandoned, while the avoidant partner can gradually increase their emotional availability without feeling overwhelmed. Setting clear expectations about alone time versus together time can prevent misunderstandings.

Anxious and Disorganized Attachment

- For the anxious partner: Understand that your partner with a disorganized attachment style may be dealing with fear, trauma, or deep-seated anxieties that affect their ability to be emotionally consistent. Be patient, but also practice setting healthy boundaries so that their unpredictability doesn't heighten your own anxiety.

- For the disorganized partner: Your anxious partner may look to you for reassurance, but your own fear of closeness might make this difficult. Acknowledge your emotional triggers and communicate with your partner about how you can work together. Therapy can help you process unresolved trauma that may be impacting your attachment style.

- Together: This can be a complex pairing because both partners have emotional needs that might feel at odds. Seek couples therapy to help navigate these dynamics, and work on establishing small, consistent acts of emotional safety. Both partners will need to build trust gradually, learning to support each other without becoming overwhelmed.

Avoidant and Disorganized Attachment

- For the avoidant partner: Recognize that your partner with a disorganized attachment style may struggle with emotional regulation due to past trauma. It's important to remain calm and patient when they seem anxious or inconsistent. Try to be emotionally available in small ways, even if it feels uncomfortable.

- For the disorganized partner: Understand that your avoidant partner's need for space is not a rejection of you. Instead of reacting with fear or anger, try to communicate your feelings when you're struggling. At the same time, work on managing your emotional triggers, ideally with the help of a therapist.

- Together: This pairing may need professional help to manage the emotional extremes between the avoidant partner's need for distance and the disorganized partner's fear of abandonment. Building trust through small, consistent actions will help both partners create a safer emotional environment. Gradual exposure to more emotional intimacy can help the avoidant partner feel less overwhelmed, while the disorganized partner can learn to manage their fears.

Anxious and Anxious Attachment

- For both partners: When both partners have an anxious attachment style, the relationship can become emotionally intense, with each partner seeking constant reassurance from the other. Be mindful of this tendency and work on building your own emotional resilience. Encourage each other to take time apart to reflect, process, and self-soothe instead of relying solely on each other for validation.

- Together: It's important to create a healthy balance of closeness and independence. Regular communication about boundaries and emotional needs can prevent the relationship from becoming too enmeshed. Couples in this pairing might benefit from focusing on building individual confidence and pursuing separate interests to reduce co-dependency.

Avoidant and Avoidant Attachment

- For both partners: If both partners have avoidant attachment styles, there may be a lack of emotional intimacy and connection, as both individuals may prefer to keep their distance. It's important to work on opening up to each other, even if it's just in small steps. Start with sharing feelings about neutral topics, and gradually work towards deeper emotional conversations.

- Together: While you both value your independence, make sure you're not neglecting the emotional connection that keeps a relationship strong. Plan intentional moments of closeness, whether through physical touch, shared activities, or conversations about your relationship goals. Create routines that allow for emotional connection while respecting your mutual need for space.

Boundaries

Boundaries are essential in any healthy relationship because they help define where one person's needs and emotions end, and the other's begin. They preserve a sense of individuality, even within the closeness of a romantic partnership. In the excitement and intimacy of a relationship, it's easy to lose sight of these boundaries. The longer you're together, the more intertwined your lives become—emotionally, physically, and mentally. This closeness can be beautiful, but without clear boundaries, it can also lead to confusion, resentment, and even burnout.

When boundaries fade, it's often because people stop prioritizing their personal space, needs, or time, especially when they feel deeply connected to their partner. Over time, they might forget to protect their emotional well-being in the desire to keep their partner happy or to avoid conflict. In many cases, this loss of boundaries becomes more significant if one or both partners haven't fully dealt with their attachment issues. Unhealed attachment wounds can make it difficult to set or maintain boundaries, especially when the fear of abandonment or rejection looms large.

Take, for example, a person with anxious attachment tendencies. They may struggle with the fear of being left behind or not being "enough" for their partner. This fear can drive them to go beyond their comfort zone, overextending emotionally, trying to please their partner at the expense of their own needs. They might push themselves to be available constantly, avoid setting limits, and sacrifice their well-being for the relationship. On the other side of the spectrum, someone with avoidant attachment might have boundaries that are too rigid. They may distance themselves emotionally, afraid that letting their partner too close will make them vulnerable to pain or disappointment. This creates a push-and-pull dynamic, where one partner might feel overwhelmed by the lack of space, while the other feels neglected or emotionally disconnected.

The health of any relationship relies on setting boundaries that balance closeness and individuality. Without clear boundaries, even the most loving partnerships can become strained over time. Boundaries foster mutual respect by ensuring that both individuals are treated as equal partners, capable of meeting each other's needs while respecting their own.

Maintaining boundaries doesn't mean you love each other less; it simply means you respect the relationship enough to maintain your own identity. In fact, when each partner knows the other's boundaries, they become more attuned to each other's emotional well-being. They learn to navigate conflicts more effectively because they understand the limits of what the other is willing or able to give at any given time.

For instance, when you and your partner understand each other's emotional boundaries, you're better able to offer the right kind of support without overstepping. You learn when your partner needs space to process their emotions and when they might need comfort. This balance creates an atmosphere of safety, where both partners can thrive emotionally and communicate more openly.

It's also important to recognize that boundaries can evolve over time. As your relationship deepens, and as each of you grows as individuals, your needs and emotional thresholds will change. Re-establishing or adjusting boundaries doesn't have to be a sign of weakness; rather, it's a necessary step to ensure that the relationship continues to grow in a healthy way. It's about honoring the person you've become, while still respecting the love you share with your partner.

Perhaps the most challenging part of boundary-setting in a relationship is recognizing when they've become blurred. Often, it takes some self-reflection to notice when you've started feeling emotionally drained or stretched too thin. Once you've acknowledged this, the next step is to have an open conversation with your partner about what needs to change. It's not about creating distance, but about ensuring that both partners feel valued and respected.

If attachment issues have been present in your relationship, it may be even more difficult to maintain these boundaries, but it's also more crucial. A person who has not fully healed from past attachment wounds may struggle to understand where their needs end and their partner's needs begin. They might project old fears and insecurities onto the relationship, making it even more challenging to navigate the emotional space between them. This is why healing those attachment wounds—whether through self-reflection, therapy, or mutual support—is key to building strong, lasting boundaries.

Boundaries ultimately create a safe space for love and trust to flourish.

Healthy VS Unhealthy Boundaries

Not all boundaries are created equal, and it's important to recognize the difference between healthy and unhealthy boundaries in relationships. Healthy boundaries are established to protect your well-being, foster mutual respect, and promote emotional growth for both partners. Unhealthy boundaries, on the other hand, may create distance, resentment, or emotional imbalance, making it difficult to sustain a loving, supportive partnership.

Healthy boundaries are based on open communication, respect, and understanding. They allow both partners to maintain their sense of individuality while still being deeply connected. For example, setting aside time for self-care or personal interests, even when you're in a relationship, is a healthy boundary. It ensures that each partner has space to nurture their own emotional well-being, which ultimately benefits the relationship as a whole. Another example of a healthy boundary might be expressing the need for emotional support without expecting your partner to "fix" all of your problems. You can share your feelings, ask for a listening ear, but also respect that your partner has their own emotional limits.

In contrast, unhealthy boundaries often arise from fear, control, or insecurity. They can look like one partner trying to dictate or limit the other's behavior in unhealthy ways. For example, setting rules that prevent your partner from spending time with friends or family is an unhealthy boundary. It's rooted in control rather than mutual respect. Another example could be using emotional withdrawal as a punishment during conflict. Withdrawing affection or giving your partner the "silent treatment" creates a power imbalance and can damage trust over time.

Unhealthy boundaries also include expecting your partner to meet all your emotional needs, which places an overwhelming burden on them. While it's natural to turn to your partner for support, relying on them as your sole source of comfort, happiness, or validation can suffocate the relationship. It's important to have multiple sources of support, whether through friendships, hobbies, or individual self-care practices.

It's equally important to understand that rigid boundaries can be as unhealthy as having no boundaries at all. A person with rigid boundaries might avoid emotional closeness, refuse to compromise, or shut down any attempt at deepening intimacy out of fear of vulnerability. For example, someone might say, "I never talk about my emotions" or "I don't need anyone's help," which, in the context of a relationship, can lead to disconnection and loneliness. On the other hand, someone with weak boundaries might consistently overextend themselves for their partner, say yes to everything out of fear of conflict, or neglect their own needs to keep the peace, which can lead to burnout and resentment.

To cultivate a healthy balance, it's essential to build flexible boundaries—ones that respect both individual needs and the needs of the relationship. This means being able to assert your needs without guilt, while also being open to compromise and understanding where your partner is coming from. Healthy boundaries are adaptable and can change as both individuals grow and evolve, ensuring that both partners feel supported, respected, and free to express themselves authentically.

For example, in a healthy relationship, you might set boundaries around communication. Perhaps you agree that during arguments, you'll both take a break if things become too heated, allowing each person time to cool down before returning to the discussion with a clearer perspective. This boundary protects the relationship from unnecessary harm, while still honoring each person's emotional process. Another example is setting limits on how much time is spent together versus time spent apart. Healthy boundaries mean that while you cherish your time together, you also recognize the importance of maintaining individual friendships, hobbies, and personal space.

Ultimately, healthy boundaries foster trust and intimacy, while unhealthy ones can erode these foundations. By staying mindful of the boundaries you set and checking in with your partner regularly, you can ensure that both of you feel respected, valued, and connected in a way that promotes long-term growth and happiness in your relationship.

Boundaries Assessment and Creation

Step 1: Reflect on Your Current Boundaries

Personal Boundaries

- *What personal space or alone time do I need to feel balanced in my relationship?*
- *Are there certain activities or hobbies I avoid because of my partner's preferences?*
- *How comfortable am I saying "no" to my partner without feeling guilty or fearful of conflict?*

Emotional Boundaries

- *Do I feel safe expressing my emotions with my partner?*
- *How often do I take responsibility for my partner's emotions or expect them to manage mine?*
- *Do I respect my partner's emotional limits, or do I push them to provide support when they're not emotionally available?*

Communication Boundaries

- *Do I feel like my voice is heard during discussions or disagreements?*
- *Are there moments when I shut down or avoid conflict instead of addressing it openly?*
- *How do I respond when my partner tries to express a need or boundary?*

Physical Boundaries

- *Do I have the space I need for myself when I need it (e.g., time to relax, work, or recharge alone)?*
- *Do I communicate clearly when I'm not comfortable with physical touch or intimacy?*
- *Am I aware of my partner's physical boundaries, and do I respect them?*

Take a moment to write down your answers in your journal. As you review them, notice any patterns or areas where boundaries might be unclear or too rigid.

Step 2: Identify Whether Boundaries are Healthy or Unhealthy

- *Is this boundary based on respect and mutual understanding, or is it rooted in fear or control?*
  Example: If you avoid certain activities because you're afraid of your partner's disapproval, this may be an unhealthy boundary rooted in fear.

- *Does this boundary allow for open communication and compromise, or is it overly rigid or non-existent?*
  Example: If you always shut down emotionally during arguments to avoid conflict, this is an unhealthy boundary that prevents growth.

- *Do these boundaries feel fair and balanced for both you and your partner, or do they primarily serve one person's needs?*
  Example: If you consistently prioritize your partner's needs while neglecting your own, this is an unhealthy, one-sided boundary.

For each boundary you listed in Step 1, mark whether it feels healthy or unhealthy and jot down why you think so.

———

PERSONAL BOUNDARIES	
PARTNER 1	PARTNER 2

EMOTIONAL BOUNDARIES	
PARTNER 1	PARTNER 2

COMMUNICATION BOUNDARIES	
PARTNER 1	PARTNER 2

PHYSICAL BOUNDARIES	
PARTNER 1	PARTNER 2

Step 3: Create New, Healthy Boundaries

Now that you've reflected on your current boundaries, it's time to establish new, healthier ones where needed. Use these guiding principles:

1. **Boundaries should respect both partners' needs.**

2. **They should be clear, specific, and communicated openly.**

3. **Healthy boundaries allow for flexibility and growth, not rigidity or avoidance.**

Ask yourself:

- *What changes can I make to create healthier boundaries in areas that feel unbalanced?*
  For example, if you realize you don't give yourself enough personal space, you might set a new boundary like, "I need one hour each day to unwind alone."

- *How can I communicate this new boundary with my partner in a constructive way?*
  Write down how you plan to introduce and explain your new boundary to your partner. Be sure to use "I" statements and avoid placing blame. Example: "I've realized I need more time for myself after work to recharge. I'd like to set aside some quiet time in the evenings so I can come back feeling refreshed."

- *What boundaries can I set to improve emotional safety and communication?*
  You might decide to set a boundary around how you argue or discuss difficult topics, such as, "When we start to feel overwhelmed, let's take a break and come back to the discussion when we're both calm."

List three to five new boundaries you'd like to establish, and how you plan to communicate them with your partner.

Step 4: Discuss Boundaries with Your Partner

Once you've reflected on your own boundaries, it's important to have a conversation with your partner to ensure mutual understanding and respect for each other's limits.

Reflection Questions After the Conversation

After you've had the guided conversation, each partner can take a few minutes to reflect privately on how the conversation went. Use these questions for personal reflection:

- *Did I feel heard and respected during the conversation? Why or why not?*
  Were there any moments where I felt defensive or misunderstood? How can I address those feelings in a calm way?
  Do the boundaries we discussed feel like they will strengthen our relationship? If not, what adjustments need to be made?
  How can I better respect my partner's boundaries moving forward?

PARTNER 1	
NEW BOUNDARY	HOW TO COMMUNICATE IT
NEW BOUNDARY	HOW TO COMMUNICATE IT
NEW BOUNDARY	HOW TO COMMUNICATE IT
NEW BOUNDARY	HOW TO COMMUNICATE IT

PARTNER 1

NEW BOUNDARY	HOW TO COMMUNICATE IT

NEW BOUNDARY	HOW TO COMMUNICATE IT

NEW BOUNDARY	HOW TO COMMUNICATE IT

NEW BOUNDARY	HOW TO COMMUNICATE IT

Creating a Safe Space

A secure environment is essential because it allows everything to flourish. In the embrace of safety, your sense of freedom grows, and with thoughtful plans built on trust, you're able to embrace life with greater confidence. In relationships, when nurtured with trust and safety, love grows naturally. A safe space allows your bond to deepen, helping both you and your partner reach your full potential together. Unfortunately, not all relationships begin in this space of security. Insecurities, childhood traumas, and fears can creep into your relationship, robbing you of the ability to trust and feel safe. These past experiences may leave you questioning the very foundation of your relationship. Trust may seem difficult to rebuild, but it's not impossible. Recognizing how past wounds affect your current relationship is the first step toward healing—both individually and together. Healing is a journey you must embark on, and it's a gift you can offer to both yourself and your relationship. Creating a safe space for each other is part of that healing process. When you prioritize safety and trust, you not only strengthen your bond but also contribute to each other's emotional well-being. A safe relationship positively impacts everything—from how you communicate to how you handle stress and even how much personal growth your relationship encourages.

The key to building a safe space is intention and effort. Here are the essential elements that can help you create a secure and nurturing environment:

1. Being Compassionate

Compassion is the foundation of emotional safety. No one wants to share their deepest thoughts and feelings with someone who isn't empathetic or understanding. By showing compassion, you reassure your partner that they can count on you for emotional support, even when you don't completely agree with their perspective.

When your partner shares their feelings, listen without judgment. Validate their emotions by acknowledging their perspective. You can say things like, "I understand why you'd feel that way," or "It makes sense that this situation is hard for you." This builds trust and emotional safety over time.

2. Building Trust

Trust is crucial for creating a safe space in a relationship. Without trust, it's nearly impossible to feel secure enough to share vulnerabilities or rely on your partner. Building trust takes time and consistency—it's about showing up, being transparent, and following through on promises.

Consistently follow through on what you say you will do, no matter how small. Over time, this will show your partner that they can rely on you. If trust has been broken, be open about your intentions to rebuild it, and have conversations about what you both need in order to feel secure moving forward.

3. Embracing Vulnerability

Vulnerability is often seen as a risk, but it's one of the most powerful ways to create a safe space in your relationship. When both partners are open about their fears, insecurities, and weaknesses, it fosters deeper emotional intimacy. However, vulnerability requires trust—without it, opening up can feel too risky.

Take the initiative by sharing something personal with your partner, such as a past hurt or a fear you're currently facing. Showing vulnerability first often encourages your partner to do the same. Over time, this mutual openness strengthens your bond and helps create a deeper connection.

4. Recognizing and Respecting Boundaries

Boundaries are an essential part of a healthy relationship. They protect both partners' emotional well-being and ensure that neither feels pressured or overwhelmed. When you respect each other's limits, you demonstrate trust, understanding, and respect.

Have open discussions about your personal boundaries—what feels comfortable for you and what doesn't. This could include emotional topics that are hard to discuss or limits on personal space and time. Respect these boundaries by never pushing your partner to talk about something before they are ready, and be mindful of giving them space when they need it.

5. Spending Quality Time Together

Creating a safe space also involves spending meaningful time together. When you make time for each other, you're reinforcing that your relationship is a priority. This shared time helps build emotional closeness, which is essential for safety and trust in a relationship.

Schedule regular quality time with your partner that allows for both fun and meaningful conversations. This could be a weekly date night, a walk together, or simply setting aside time to talk without distractions. Use this time to check in with your partner about how they are feeling, discuss any challenges, and share positive experiences.

Trust-Building Activities

Trust is the foundation of a healthy relationship. This little section includes activities that help to build and reinforce trust between partners, essential for a strong, resilient partnership.

Blindfold Trust Walk: One partner is blindfolded while the other guides them through a series of simple tasks or a short walk. This exercise requires the blindfolded partner to trust their partner's guidance completely.

Share Vulnerabilities: Set aside time to share something vulnerable with your partner—a fear, a worry, or a past experience. The listening partner's role is to provide support without judgment.

Commitment Check-In: Discuss your commitments to each other and reaffirm them. This can be as simple as verbalizing your dedication to the relationship or setting new goals together.

Trust Journal: Both partners keep a trust journal for a week, noting moments when they felt trust was strengthened or weakened. At the end of the week, discuss your entries together.

———

Week 3

Effective Communication

Relationships are built between two individuals who, inevitably, have differences—in their views, personal experiences, and ways of interacting with the world. No two people are exactly alike, and once you discover your shared values, you will naturally encounter areas where you differ.

One thing that almost everyone agrees on is the crucial role of communication in any relationship. Each day, in various ways, we communicate. Whether it's lending your voice to speak out against an injustice, offering support to friends and family, or bringing a smile to someone's face with a simple joke, communication is constant. Even if you consider yourself calm, reserved, or open-minded, you're always conveying something. We've come to understand the power of effective communication and how it shapes the different aspects of our lives.

For example, during a job interview, you don't just speak for the sake of it—you aim to provide clear and convincing answers. When comforting a friend through a tough time, you choose your words carefully, offering support that resonates. Similarly, as you enter the next phase of your relationship, it's important to extend that same level of thoughtfulness and grace to your partner through effective communication.

There's a common misconception that couples get stuck in misunderstandings because they don't talk enough. However, the truth is that simply speaking isn't enough. Communication goes beyond just exchanging words. To truly connect, couples need to unravel the nuances of effective communication—making sure both partners understand the deeper meaning behind their words and are equipped to resolve differences in a constructive way.

The ultimate purpose of communication in a relationship is to bridge the gap between two different worlds—to understand your partner's perspective, even when it differs from your own. Effective communication involves not only telling your story but also listening and absorbing your partner's ideas and viewpoints. Picture yourself in a complex puzzle or mystery game: to find the solution, you need to pay close attention to every detail. Similarly, in a relationship, every word, gesture, tone, or even silence can hold significant meaning. To truly understand your partner, it's essential to recognize and appreciate their unique personality, background, and experiences.

Effective communication is the means by which diverse ideas and perspectives are brought into alignment. And like any meaningful process, it requires intentional effort and practice. Incorporating practical strategies into your everyday communication—such as empathy exercises, active listening, and emotional awareness—can significantly improve the way you and your partner interact, ensuring that both of you feel heard and understood.

Active Listening

Actively listening to your spouse takes more than just hearing them speak. This time around, you are involved and ready to engage them on the topic they bring up emotionally. To do this, you must become more reflective on how you respond. With that, you can effectively prevent misunderstanding and constant friction because each partner is not communicating to win the argument; instead, the listener is ready to reflect on the issue and offer emotional support through a reflective response.

Let's imagine a situation where your partner expressed frustration about how you treated them or handled something they did. For instance, your partner making better financial decisions may require cutting some expenses, which may not sit right with you the first time you hear about it. When it is time to discuss this topic, they may see your lack of support as an attempt to frustrate the better plan they made, and this may prompt them to comment like: "I see that you don't appreciate the plan I made about XYZ."

Learning to give reflective responses will require you to validate their feelings while expressing your concern about the decision. This will also allow them to express their feelings about the situation. Response like: "It is not that I do not appreciate your effect. I understand that you have our best interest at heart, but I am only worried that this plan may affect ABC."

From here, you and your partner have moved from internal disagreement to a point where expressing your thoughts and feelings freely and clearly is possible without resulting in argument, fighting, and name-calling.

Expressing Needs and Feelings

Being the person who communicates, the person who starts a conversation around a topic, and the one who cannot wait until a disagreement is settled can be a little too overwhelming. However, if you are in a relationship with someone who handles certain situations silently, cultivating a habit of expressing needs and feelings can help validate their feelings and make them feel safe. It is essential to know that the fact that your partner does not communicate as often as you would like doesn't always mean that the relationship doesn't matter to them. Being confident in your love and trying even to have a better experience can take the form of helping your partner break out of their shell by offering more assurance and safety.

You do not always be the person who talks; instead, you can replace that with a regular communication ritual.

Set a 15-minute check-in time when you and your partner can discuss life outside your relationship. This opens the door to discussing the external stressors that may affect your relationship. Pick any topic from how your day went, how stressful work was, or how annoying something was. Anything that allows both of you to express your feelings and needs. The result is not to fix a problem but to create a comfortable atmosphere that enables partners to see through each other's experiences.

The Power of Nonverbal Communication

Sometimes, what is left unsaid can be as powerful as what was articulate, and sometimes, it can be more consequential. Your partner is someone who must care about your feelings, and this can make them omit saying certain things. However, you can communicate better by paying attention to the non-verbal cues. Sometimes, you must focus on the tone or the body language to understand the message they are trying to convey. Not every OK signals agreement and understanding that can help you manage your relationship better.

For instance, if your partner is uncomfortable speaking about a topic, this may be the time to sit back and focus on their body language instead of what is being said. Doing this allows you to give responses that further reassure them of your readiness to hear all about their thoughts, take relevant criticisms, and navigate towards finding a mutually beneficial solution.

Seek Clarification

Assumptions are the greatest destroyer of relationships because they breed misunderstanding, and misunderstanding breeds hatred. Can you see how that spirals into a big issue?

The truth is that when you assume you know something, you naturally ignore the other person's perspective. Yes, knowing your partner is a prerequisite for building a healthy relationship where trust thrives, but this does not require that you assume the role of a know-it-all figure. You won't be able to figure everything out independently, so asking questions to clarify misunderstandings is a grace you must be willing to offer your relationship.

In every situation, instead of presuming your partner's thoughts or inferring a self-constructed conclusion, ask questions to get clarification. For instance, you may think your partner's silence means a gradual loss of interest, but they may struggle with personal issues. Asking open-ended questions in such a situation allows you to take in some of their trouble and take further steps to resolve what may be troubling them.

Questions like, "I notice you didn't say a word at the party. Was there something you didn't like there, or is there something else on your mind lately," make it easy to open up communication on the silence that is bothering you without focusing on the fact that their silence made you feel some way.

————

Find the Right Time for Every Topic

Finding the right time is as important as learning to communicate. At the right time, you get the best out of your communication. Also, learning about timing can help you discern what topic to discuss and when. For instance, discussing a serious issue with your partner when they are most stressed can lead to ineffective communication. It is crucial to understand that the essence of communicating is to say your part of the story and give the other person the chance to air their views. Hence, it is essential that the time is comfortable for both parties and the topic is appropriate.

Use a calm atmosphere to discuss salient relationship troubles, use a relaxing moment to open up an emotional dialogue that brings you closer to your partner, and use the stressed time to discuss things that allow you to offer each other support and empathy to keep navigating the hurdles of live in your personal space.

Avoiding Blame and Criticism

Effective communication is far from finding who did what. It is not about who should take the blame but more about how to resolve the problem. Avoiding blame is not usually easy when you know somewhere within you that you are right, but the essence of communicating with your partner is not to be correct but to find common ground where you can both agree.

An open and safe communication space is not judgmental; it is a space where both partners work together to preserve and improve the relationship. You will not always agree on every topic, but you can learn to constructively resolve issues without belittling each other perspectives or ideas.

When expressing yourself, employing an "I" statement is an efficient way to avoid placing blame on your partner while passing across your message effectively. For instance, saying, "I feel frustrated when you do XYZ," is a better way of expressing your needs and feelings than saying, "You always take me for granted when you do XYZ."

Active Listening

Active listening is key to understanding your partner fully. This practice focuses on listening without interruptions, allowing you to tune into both the words and emotions your partner is sharing. Find a time when both of you can be undistracted and focused. Take turns talking and listening. As one speaks, the other fully concentrates, reflecting back what they've heard to ensure clarity. Afterward, discuss how the exercise felt. Was there a deeper sense of being heard?

"I" Statements

When conversations start with "You always..." or "You never...," it often leads to defensiveness and conflict. Using "I" statements shifts the focus onto your feelings without placing blame. Instead of framing a complaint as something your partner did wrong, express how you felt in the situation. For example, "I feel upset when plans change last minute because I need time to adjust. I would appreciate a heads-up next time." After each person shares, the other listens without interruption and responds with understanding. This helps foster constructive, rather than confrontational, dialogue.

Daily Check-In

A daily check-in is a simple yet powerful way to stay connected with your partner, even during hectic times. Set aside a few minutes each day—whether over morning coffee or before bed—to ask each other open-ended questions like, "What was the highlight of your day?" and, "Is there anything on your mind?" This exercise is about sharing, listening, and being present for each other. Conclude each check-in with an expression of appreciation, reinforcing positive feelings and connection between you.

Reflective Listening

Reflective listening helps partners feel heard and validated. Choose a recent topic that may have been challenging or unclear. One person shares their thoughts and emotions around the issue, while the other listens and paraphrases what they heard. For example, "It sounds like you felt excluded when your opinion wasn't considered." This way, the listener demonstrates understanding, and the speaker has the chance to confirm or clarify. Once both partners feel understood, switch roles.

Empathy Exercise

Empathy strengthens emotional intimacy by helping you understand your partner's feelings. Choose a recent situation where one of you expressed strong emotions. As your partner shares how they felt, focus on understanding their emotional experience. Try to step into their shoes, reflecting back what you believe they felt, like "It seems like you were really hurt when I missed the event because you felt unimportant." Confirm whether this was accurate and ask if there's more to understand. Switch roles once each person has had a chance to be heard.

Week 4

Conflict Resolution

Conflict is inevitable in every relationship, and how you manage and resolve it will greatly influence the long-term health and stability of your partnership. Disagreements are a natural part of being together, and it's essential to accept that no matter how strong your love or how solid your foundation, conflict is unavoidable.

Instead of focusing on what went wrong during a disagreement, it's more productive to concentrate on how to make things right moving forward. This is why understanding different conflict resolution strategies and recognizing how your partner handles conflict are key to building a healthy relationship.

Your relationship, shaped by your unique backgrounds and experiences, can thrive despite these inevitable challenges. Conflicts arise in all human interactions, and learning how to navigate them is a crucial skill. Resolving disputes often requires more than just offering an apology—it demands active collaboration from both partners to truly fix underlying issues and allow the relationship to flourish.

Each conflict you resolve opens the door to a deeper understanding of your partner. It's an opportunity to learn more about their preferences, their values, and the topics that resonate with them. You'll gain insight into how they communicate and what issues they feel strongly about, as well as what they prefer to avoid. The goal of conflict resolution is not to prevent disagreements entirely but to ensure they don't keep resurfacing over the same issues. Each resolution teaches you something new, revealing truths about your relationship and reinforcing the idea that different approaches can lead to better outcomes.

Ultimately, the peace you seek is on the other side of the disputes you work to resolve. Conflict resolution is essential for creating a harmonious and fulfilling relationship. When you handle disagreements constructively, you create a more loving and supportive environment for both partners, allowing your relationship to become a better place for the two of you to grow together.

Conflict Resolution Styles

Everyone approaches conflict differently, which is why you and your partner might not always see eye to eye when it comes to resolving disagreements. Understanding each other's unique conflict resolution style is crucial because it not only reveals more about your partner's approach to handling difficult situations, but it also provides insight into areas that might need improvement. Additionally, it helps predict the outcome of conflicts and offers ways to navigate them more effectively.

Here are some of the most common conflict resolution styles and practical tips for handling each:

1. The Avoider: Avoiders tend to shy away from confrontation, often withdrawing when conflict arises. They may feel overwhelmed by the potential consequences of expressing their feelings and believe that avoiding the issue will prevent further harm. While this style can defuse immediate tension, it often leads to unresolved issues that eventually resurface, causing resentment to build up over time.

Encourage the avoider to open up in a low-pressure environment. Use gentle language and avoid accusations. Frame the conversation as a way to improve the relationship, not to assign blame. Set small goals to address one issue at a time, making conflict feel less overwhelming.

2. The Accommodator: Accommodators prioritize maintaining harmony and often put their partner's needs above their own. While this can create temporary peace, it may come at the cost of their own emotional fulfillment. Over time, accommodating too much can lead to frustration or resentment, especially if the individual feels their own needs are consistently overlooked.

If you or your partner tends to accommodate too often, practice speaking up about your own needs. It's helpful to remind yourself that a healthy relationship requires both partners to feel valued and heard. Balance is key—encouraging your partner to express their desires as well can lead to more fulfilling outcomes for both of you.

3. The Competitor: Competitors view conflict as a win-lose situation. They tend to focus on "winning" the argument rather than finding a resolution that benefits both partners. While this approach can be useful in situations that require quick decision-making, it can be damaging in relationships where mutual compromise is more important than being right.

If competition drives your conflict, try shifting the focus from proving who's right to understanding how you both feel. Approach conflict with curiosity rather than a desire to win. Ask open-ended questions like, "What's most important to you in this situation?" This helps create space for empathy and mutual understanding.

4. The Collaborator: The collaborator sees conflict as an opportunity to strengthen the relationship. They view disagreements as a chance to understand their partner better and work towards a solution that benefits both parties. Collaboration fosters healthy communication and ensures that neither partner feels neglected or dominated.

If you and your partner already lean toward collaboration, keep up the good work by scheduling regular check-ins to discuss any small issues before they grow into larger problems. Collaborators can further strengthen their approach by practicing active listening and ensuring both partners have the opportunity to voice their thoughts equally.

———

5. The Compromiser: Compromisers aim to find middle ground. They focus on quickly identifying the root cause of the disagreement and are willing to make concessions to reach an agreement. While this can be an effective and swift way to resolve conflict, it's important to note that compromise can sometimes leave both partners feeling unsatisfied if their needs aren't fully addressed.

When compromise is the preferred method, ensure that both partners feel their core needs are being met. Ask, "Is there anything about this solution that doesn't sit well with you?" This helps avoid superficial compromises that don't truly resolve the underlying issue.

How the Four Conflict Styles Can Work Together

By understanding how these styles can complement each other, you and your partner can de-velop a more flexible and adaptive approach to resolving conflicts. The key is to recognize the value in each style and learn how to apply them in a way that strengthens your relationship ra-ther than creating friction. Embracing this balance will help you both navigate disagreements more effectively and foster a deeper connection built on mutual respect and understanding.

Avoidant and Collaborative: While the Avoidant style seeks to minimize conflict, the Collabora-tive style actively seeks resolution through open dialogue. These styles can balance each other by ensuring that not every disagreement turns into a lengthy discussion, while also ensuring that important issues are addressed. The Avoidant partner can learn to engage more with con-flicts when they arise, while the Collaborative partner can practice patience, allowing space for their partner to process before engaging in deep discussions.

Compromising and Competitive: The Compromising style is great for finding quick solutions, while the Competitive style ensures that essential needs and boundaries are asserted. When these two styles work together, the relationship benefits from a balance between assertive-ness and flexibility. The Compromising partner can help temper the Competitive partner's drive, ensuring that resolutions are fair and considerate of both parties. Meanwhile, the Com-petitive partner can ensure that critical issues are not glossed over and that both partners ad-vocate for their needs.

Collaborative and Compromising: Collaboration and Compromise are often seen as the most relationship-friendly conflict styles. When these two styles are used together, they can ensure that both partners feel heard and valued. Collaboration focuses on finding solutions that fully satisfy both partners, while Compromise ensures that decisions can be made even when per-fect solutions aren't possible. The Compromising partner can keep things moving forward, while the Collaborative partner ensures that the resolutions are meaningful and not just quick fixes.

Avoidant and Competitive: At first glance, Avoidant and Competitive styles might seem at odds, but they can actually complement each other. The Competitive partner's assertiveness can draw out important issues that the Avoidant partner might otherwise shy away from ad-dressing. On the other hand, the Avoidant partner can help temper conflicts by stepping back when emotions run high, allowing both partners to cool down before re-engaging. Together, they can navigate conflicts without allowing them to escalate unnecessarily.

Avoidant and Compromising: The Avoidant partner may prefer to avoid confrontation, while the Compromising partner is more open to negotiating. Together, these styles can create a dynam-ic where minor conflicts are peacefully sidestepped, and more significant issues are addressed through compromise. The Compromising partner can gently encourage the Avoidant partner to engage in discussions when necessary, ensuring that issues don't go unresolved.

Collaborative and Avoidant: While Collaborators aim to resolve conflicts fully, Avoid-ant part-ners may shy away from addressing issues head-on. In this dynamic, the Collaborative partner can take the lead in gently bringing up issues that need resolution, while respecting the Avoidant partner's need for space. Over time, the Collaborative partner can help create a safe environment where the Avoidant partner feels more comfortable engaging in conflict resolu-tion.

Compromising and Avoidant: In this mix, the Compromising partner might be the one to initi-ate discussions and suggest solutions, while the Avoidant partner could be more receptive to these suggestions, as they don't require direct confrontation. This pairing can be effective in maintaining harmony, though it's essential for the Compromising partner to ensure that the Avoidant partner's voice is heard in the decision-making process.

Competitive and Collaborative: Competitors are focused on asserting their needs, while Collab-orators seek win-win solutions. When these styles work together, the Competitive partner en-sures that critical issues are addressed with determination, while the Collaborative partner works to find a resolution that satisfies both parties. The key to success here is for the Compet-itive partner to remain open to collaborative strategies, recognizing that their needs can be met in a way that also respects their partner's needs.

Conflict Style Quiz

For each of the following scenarios, choose the response that best reflects how you would typically react.

1. **When your partner disagrees with you on an important issue, you:**

    A) Avoid the topic to prevent an argument.

    B) Try to find a middle ground that satisfies both of you.

    C) Stand firm on your viewpoint and argue your case.

    D) Let your partner have their way to keep the peace.

    E) Work together to find a solution that fully addresses both perspectives.

2. **If you feel your partner isn't listening to you, you:**

    A) Stop talking about the issue and withdraw.

    B) Suggest a compromise to move the discussion forward.

    C) Insist that they listen to your point of view.

    D) Quietly go along with their ideas instead.

    E) Calmly explain your feelings and ask for their attention.

3. **When you notice your partner is upset about something, you:**

    A) Give them space until they are ready to talk.

    B) Offer a solution that might help both of you.

    C) Confront them to address the issue head-on.

    D) Reassure them and let them know you're on their side.

    E) Ask them to share their feelings and listen carefully.

4. **In an argument, your primary goal is to:**

    A) Avoid making the situation worse by staying quiet.

    B) Find a compromise that stops the argument.

    C) Convince your partner that you're right.

    D) Make sure your partner is not upset.

    E) Resolve the issue in a way that benefits both of you.

5. **When your partner brings up a complaint, you:**

    A) Change the subject to avoid conflict.

    B) Try to meet them halfway.

C) Defend yourself and explain why they are wrong.

D) Apologize and try to make things right immediately.

E) Discuss the complaint openly to find a fair solution.

Scoring and Interpretation

- **Mostly A's: Avoidant** - You tend to steer clear of conflicts, preferring to avoid confrontation whenever possible. While this can prevent immediate disputes, unresolved issues may linger.

- **Mostly B's: Compromising** - You seek middle-ground solutions that partially satisfy both parties. This style can be effective but sometimes leads to neither partner fully getting what they need.

- **Mostly C's: Competitive** - You tend to confront conflicts directly, often with the goal of winning the argument. This can be effective in standing your ground but may create a power struggle.

- **Mostly D's: Accommodating** - You prioritize your partner's needs over your own, often yielding to avoid conflict. While this keeps the peace, it may lead to your own needs being unmet.

- **Mostly E's: Collaborative** - You strive to address both your own and your partner's needs, aiming for win-win solutions. This is the most constructive style but requires time and effort from both partners.

Discuss Your Results: Once you've identified your primary conflict style, share your findings with your partner. Talk about how your styles complement or clash with each other and brainstorm ways to adapt your approaches to resolve conflicts more effectively.

PARTNE 1:

PARTNER 2:

Strategies for Effective Conflict Resolution

Navigating conflicts with your partner requires more than knowing your style; sometimes, you have to employ strategies that allow you and your partner to cooperate as you learn to resolve rising disagreements. Here are some strategies to get the best out of conflicts.

Active Listening

One of the most important skills in conflict resolution is active listening. Instead of preparing a response or trying to "win" the conversation, focus on fully engaging with what your partner is saying. By actively listening, you're showing that you care about how they feel and trying to understand their perspective. This reflective approach gives you the chance to summarize what your partner has shared, helping to identify what can be done to improve the situation and make them feel heard.

Reflective Response

A reflective response involves repeating back what your partner has said, validating their perspective, and offering your insight. For example, you might say, "It sounds like you're frustrated because I haven't been doing XYZ. I understand why you feel that way." This technique ensures that your partner feels heard and acknowledged, paving the way for greater empathy and compassion. It also allows for deeper understanding of your partner's feelings and opens the door to resolving the issue.

Empathizing

Resolving conflict from a place of understanding rather than agreement is key. Even if you don't fully agree with your partner's perspective, it's important to validate their feelings. You might say something like, "I can see why that would make you feel bad. I understand how important XYZ is to you." Empathy reassures your partner that their feelings are valued and important to you. This supportive environment helps deescalate tension and builds trust, strengthening the bond between you both.

Identifying Shared Goals

During disagreements, it's helpful to identify shared goals and confirm them with your partner. For instance, you could say, "It's clear we both want XYZ. How about we work together to achieve that?" Finding common ground creates a space for collaboration rather than conflict. When both partners see that their desires are aligned, it becomes easier to work together toward a mutually beneficial solution, fostering a sense of partnership and teamwork.

Taking a Break

If an argument becomes too heated, it's sometimes best to suggest taking a break. This doesn't mean ignoring or dismissing your partner; instead, it allows both of you to cool down and reflect. You might suggest, "Let's take a break and discuss this later when we're both calmer." Taking time out from a disagreement helps reduce anger and prevents either partner from saying hurtful things in the heat of the moment. When you return to the conversation, you can address the issue more thoughtfully and calmly.

Resolving It Together

Once both partners have expressed their perspectives calmly, don't leave the issue unresolved. Collaborating on solutions is key. For example, you could say, "I know XYZ is important to both of us, so let's brainstorm some ideas together to handle it effectively." By working together to resolve the problem, you foster mutual respect and equality in the relationship. This cooperative approach makes it easier for both partners to compromise, apologize, and work together to move forward.

Apologizing and Forgiving

Apologizing sincerely and showing a commitment to change is essential in conflict resolution. When you apologize, make sure you acknowledge what went wrong and express your desire to handle things better in the future. For instance, "I'm sorry for making that decision without consulting you. I'll make sure to include you next time." Apologizing and forgiving allow for healing and growth, as the apologizing partner shows their dedication to change, and the forgiving partner sees that commitment.

Recognizing Your Partner's Conflict Resolution Style

Now that you are familiar with different conflict resolution styles and can pick one or two strategies to resolve conflict effectively, it's important to take this a step further by understanding your partner's conflict resolution style as well. This starts by observing how they typically approach disagreements. Reflect on past arguments to notice patterns: Do they tend to withdraw or avoid the issue altogether? Do they approach every argument with a win-or-lose mindset, perhaps even making you feel inadequate just to prove a point? Or are they more inclined to communicate calmly and resolve matters collaboratively?

Once you've identified some of these patterns, it's time to communicate openly about your conflict resolution preferences. Share how you both like to approach disagreements and reflect on how your respective styles impact the relationship. This kind of open dialogue can highlight areas where your current approaches might be lacking and reveal opportunities for growth. In these conversations, flexibility is key. You and your partner must be willing to adapt, adjusting your approach where necessary to foster a healthier, more constructive dynamic.

For instance, if your partner tends to withdraw during conflicts, it's important not to push them into confrontation. Instead, help create a safe space by approaching the conversation in a non-threatening, gentle manner that encourages them to express their feelings. This kind of understanding and flexibility strengthens your relationship, allowing for better communication and conflict resolution.

As part of this process, set aside time for an open discussion where you can talk through your points of view and fill the table in the next page.

HOW DO THEY USUALLY APPROACH CONFLICT?	
PARTNER 1:	PARTNER 2:

HOW CAN YOU BOTH ADAPT FOR A BETTER OUTCOME?

HOW DO THEY COMMUNICATE DURING DISAGREEMENTS?	
PARTNER 1:	PARTNER 2:

HOW CAN YOU BOTH ADAPT FOR A BETTER OUTCOME?

WHAT DO THEY TYPICALLY NEED DURING CONFLICTS?

PARTNER 1:	PARTNER 2:

HOW CAN YOU BOTH ADAPT FOR A BETTER OUTCOME?

HOW DO THEY RESPOND TO DIFFERENT CONFLICT RESOLUTION STRATEGIES?

PARTNER 1:	PARTNER 2:

HOW CAN YOU BOTH ADAPT FOR A BETTER OUTCOME?

WHAT TRIGGERS THEM DURING DISAGREEMENTS?

PARTNER 1:	PARTNER 2:

HOW CAN YOU BOTH ADAPT FOR A BETTER OUTCOME?

WHAT CONFLICT RESOLUTION METHOD WORKS BEST FOR THEM?

PARTNER 1:	PARTNER 2:

HOW CAN YOU BOTH ADAPT FOR A BETTER OUTCOME?

Collaborative Problem-Solving in Action

Now that you've learned the core elements of collaborative problem-solving, it's time to put them into practice. This exercise will guide you and your partner through resolving an ongoing conflict in your relationship. The goal here is not just to "win" or settle an argument but to strengthen your bond and learn how to approach future disagreements more effectively.

Step 1: Select an Ongoing Conflict

Start by choosing a conflict that has recently caused tension between you and your partner. It could be something small that keeps coming up or a more significant issue that's been harder to resolve. Make sure both of you agree on the issue you want to work through.

ISSUE:

Step 2: Define the Problem Together

Begin by sitting down and allowing both partners to communicate how they feel about the conflict. Avoid blaming or interrupting each other during this step. Instead, focus on identifying the core issue from both perspectives. Ask each other:

How does this problem affect you?

PARTENR 1:

PARTENR 2:

Why do you think this issue keeps arising?

PARTENR 1:

PARTENR 2:

Step 3: Clarify Any Misunderstandings

Next, ask clarifying questions to ensure that both of you fully understand each other's perspectives. This step helps summarize the key points of your discussion and avoids misunderstandings down the line. Ask questions like:

Can you explain what you meant when you said...?

PARTENR 1:

PARTENR 2:

How do you think I could have handled that differently?

PARTENR 1:

PARTENR 2:

Step 4: Identify Common Goals

Now that you have a clearer understanding of the problem, work together to identify mutual goals. What do you both want to achieve by resolving this conflict? Finding common ground is critical because it reminds both partners that you're on the same team, working toward a shared outcome.

What do we both want out of this situation?

PARTENR 1:

PARTENR 2:

How can resolving this problem benefit both of us?
PARTENR 1:

PARTENR 2:

Step 5: Discuss Desired Outcomes

Once you've identified your common goals, discuss the specific outcomes you both desire from the resolution. What would make each of you feel satisfied with the resolution? This is a good time to listen carefully to each other's needs.

What does an ideal resolution look like for you?
PARTENR 1:

PARTENR 2:

How can we make sure both of us feel valued in the outcome?
PARTENR 1:

PARTENR 2:

Step 6: Curate Possible Solutions

Now it's time to brainstorm solutions. Create a list of potential ways to resolve the conflict, allowing both partners to contribute ideas without judgment. Let your partner express their thoughts fully, and write down everything, even if some ideas seem impractical at first. After brainstorming, work together to refine the list into a few viable options.

Step 7: Combine Your Ideas

Review your lists of possible solutions and explore how they could work together. Discuss which ideas are realistic and which may need to be refined. The goal is to find common ground that works for both of you.

How can we combine these solutions to meet both of our needs?

PARTENR 1:

PARTENR 2:

Are there any adjustments we can make to ensure this works for both of us?

PARTENR 1:

PARTENR 2:

Step 8: Evaluate the Solutions

Take some time to evaluate the solutions you've come up with. Consider the pros and cons of each idea, and reflect on how each one could impact your relationship. Ask questions like:

How will this solution make things better for both of us?

PARTENR 1:

PARTENR 2:

What challenges might we face in implementing this solution?

PARTENR 1:

PARTENR 2:

Step 9: Develop an Action Plan

Once you've chosen the most suitable solution, it's time to develop an action plan. This is where you get specific. What are the exact steps you'll both take to implement the solution? Be clear about timelines, deadlines, and responsibilities.

What specific steps will we take to resolve this issue?

PARTENR 1:

PARTENR 2:

When will we check in on our progress to see how it's working?

PARTENR 1:

PARTENR 2:

Step 10: Define Steps and Responsibilities

Now that you've created an action plan, it's time to outline who will be responsible for each step. This ensures accountability and helps both partners feel invested in the solution.

ROLE PARTENR 1:

EXPECTATION PARTENR 1:

ROLE PARTENR 2:

EXPECTATION PARTENR 2:

Step 11: Communicate Regularly

Set aside time to check in with each other regularly to see how the solution is working. Make sure these conversations happen in a calm and supportive environment. Ask each other:

- *How is this solution working for you so far?*
- *Is there anything we need to adjust to make it work better?*

Step 12: Reflect and Learn

Finally, take time to reflect on what you've learned through this process. What went well? What could you improve on next time? This reflection will help you both learn from the experience and apply those lessons to future disagreements. Discuss:

What did we learn about each other during this process?

PARTENR 1:

PARTENR 2:

How can we improve our approach to conflict resolution in the future?

PARTENR 1:

PARTENR 2:

Role-Playing Scenarios

Role-playing can be a helpful way to practice resolving conflicts in a safe setting. Pick a typical conflict, such as a disagreement about daily routines or chores. One of you plays yourself, while the other steps into their usual role or even switches roles to see things from the other's perspective.

Respond naturally to the situation, but aim to use the communication tools you've been learning, like "I" statements or reflective listening. After a few minutes, pause and reflect. Discuss how it felt—were unexpected emotions triggered? Did you gain any new insights about your response or perspective?

If you're both comfortable, switch roles and replay the scenario, this time from the opposite perspective. This can deepen your understanding of your partner's experience and reveal any unconscious habits or patterns.

After both rounds, debrief together. Discuss what strategies worked, where things got stuck, and how you can apply these role-playing insights to real-life conflicts, making them less heated and more constructive.

Time-Out Strategy

In the heat of an argument, taking a "time-out" can help prevent escalation. Choose a common topic that tends to cause tension, such as finances or household tasks, and agree on a signal to pause the conversation if needed.

Choose a topic that tends to trigger emotions, such as finances or household responsibilities. Schedule a time when both of you are calm and ready to approach the subject thoughtfully.

Before starting, agree on a signal—a word or gesture—that either partner can use if the discussion becomes too intense. This signal is a cue to pause, and both partners must respect it once it's given.

During the conversation, remember the goal is not to "win" but to understand each other. If tensions rise, use the time-out signal. During the break, relax and reflect—don't rehearse rebuttals. You might take a walk, practice deep breathing, or jot down your thoughts. The aim is to return to the conversation with a clearer, calmer mindset.

When you resume, share any insights or reflections you had during the time-out. This can help reset the tone and encourage a more balanced discussion. Afterward, reflect on how well the time-out worked. Did it help diffuse tension? What could be improved next time? This reflection will make the time-out strategy even more effective in managing future conflicts.

Week 5

Connection & Affection

While many factors contribute to the success of a relationship, the emotional connection and affection shared between partners are at the heart of romantic love. These elements create a dynamic interplay of feelings that make the heart beat faster. However, the initial spark in a relationship doesn't stay the same forever. If left unattended, it can fade over time due to life's challenges, external stressors, and differences in life choices. That's why rekindling your love is just as important as falling in love in the first place.

In long-term relationships, emotional connection is often the first thing that fades if it's not nurtured. Life's demands—whether it's work, family, or other responsibilities—can create distance, making it easy for partners to fall into routines where they focus more on logistics than on each other. The excitement that once came from discovering new things about each other is gradually replaced by familiarity, and without conscious effort, the emotional bond that once felt effortless can start to weaken.

Building and maintaining a deep connection in a romantic relationship is not easy. It requires more than just hoping your partner will always love you or that your own feelings will remain unchanged. It's about consciously choosing to nurture the relationship. Together, you and your partner must focus on how you treat each other, invest in spending quality time, and create an environment where love can thrive. Every time you keep promises, show commitment, share dreams or fears, express your needs, and communicate openly, you reinforce trust and reliability in your relationship. These actions naturally help your love grow stronger.

Attuning to each other's feelings and fostering a deep emotional connection—one that seamlessly leads to physical touch and intimacy—is essential. The strength of your connection often determines how well you can navigate through disagreements and challenges, allowing both of you to resonate with each other on a deeper level.

In every meaningful romantic relationship, emotional and physical connections are intertwined, with each one enhancing the other. Both are essential for couples to experience a fulfilling and satisfying love life. Understanding the importance of both emotional and physical connections is the first step toward deepening the bond you share with your partner.

Emotional connection creates a safe space where trust can flourish, allowing you to share your fears, past experiences, and vulnerabilities without fear of judgment. This trust becomes a cornerstone of your relationship, forming a solid foundation upon which everything else can grow.

A strong emotional bond also fosters mutual understanding. When you're emotionally connected to your partner, it becomes easier to navigate conflicts with empathy, compassion, and emotional support. Physical connection, in turn, becomes a language of its own—communicating the depth of the emotional bond between you and your partner. As your emotional connection deepens, physical intimacy naturally follows, becoming more than just an act but a way of making your partner feel wanted, seen, and cherished. During challenging or anxious times, a comforting touch can offer reassurance and remind your partner of your unwavering support.

It's important to remember that physical connection is just as crucial as emotional connection. While an emotional bond often lays the groundwork for physical intimacy, the physical connection strengthens and deepens that emotional bond over time. Physical touch, whether it's kissing, cuddling, or hugging, releases oxytocin, which boosts feelings of closeness and helps relieve stress. In this way, physical touch helps your love grow, enriching both your emotional and physical relationship.

Emotional Bonding Self-Assessment

Take some time to reflect on the following questions. Answer them honestly, either by writing them in your journal or discussing them with your partner. This self-assessment will help you recognize where you stand emotionally and identify areas where you can grow.

How often do I feel emotionally connected to my partner?
Reflect on the times you've felt closest to your partner. Are these moments frequent or rare? What specific actions or behaviors contribute to those feelings?

PARTNER 1

PARNER 2

Do I feel comfortable sharing my fears, dreams, and vulnerabilities with my partner?
Think about the level of comfort you have when opening up. If there's hesitation, why do you think that is? What would make you feel safer?

PARTNER 1

PARNER 2

How well do I listen to my partner's feelings and concerns?

Consider how often you actively listen without interrupting or offering solutions. Do you make space for your partner's emotions?

PARTNER 1

PARNER 2

Do I make an effort to spend quality time with my partner?

Evaluate the time you dedicate to being together without distractions. How does that time affect your emotional connection?

PARTNER 1

PARNER 2

How often do I initiate physical touch or intimacy in my relationship?

Reflect on the role of physical touch in your relationship. Do you feel it helps you bond, or is it something that feels neglected?

_____

PARTNER 1

PARNER 2

Is there anything holding me back from fully trusting my partner?

Identify any barriers that may be preventing you from trusting your partner completely. Have past experiences influenced this?

PARTNER 1

PARNER 2

What does emotional bonding mean to me personally?

Define what emotional bonding looks like for you. How do you want to feel emotionally connected in your relationship, and how do you envision that bond growing?

PARTNER 1

PARNER 2

Daily Practices for Emotional Bonding

Emotional bonding is the foundation of a deep connection between partners, where understanding, trust, love, and vulnerability are woven together. However, creating and sustaining this bond doesn't always happen naturally in every relationship. Even when we understand its importance, many couples still struggle to form and maintain a meaningful emotional connection.

You may wonder why emotional bonding should be a daily focus in your relationship, or perhaps you feel uneasy acknowledging that this vital element is lacking. It's even more challenging when couples don't realize that their recurring disagreements are often a symptom of a weak emotional bond. To help you navigate the challenges of building or strengthening this connection, let's explore some practical ways to enhance emotional bonding with your partner.

First, it's important to truly understand what emotional bonding is. It goes beyond simply loving someone—it's about sharing your deepest thoughts and feelings without fear of judgment or rejection. This level of connection requires vulnerability and a willingness to be emotionally open with your partner. However, it can be uncomfortable at first, especially if you're not used to sharing your innermost thoughts.

One of the most effective ways to foster emotional bonding is through open and honest communication. Trusting someone with your story isn't always easy, especially if your relationship began in a casual setting or has evolved quickly. But if you want to form a strong bond, you have to move past the discomfort and learn to express your feelings with sincerity. This doesn't mean oversharing all at once, but rather taking small steps toward deeper conversations.

Spending quality time together is another essential practice for emotional bonding. When you make time for your partner regularly, you create an atmosphere of comfort and security. Sharing your dreams, fears, and future plans not only helps your partner understand you better, but it also gives them the space to open up and be vulnerable in return. This daily practice allows your relationship to deepen naturally.

Physical intimacy is also a key factor in emotional bonding. Simple physical acts like cuddling, kissing, or even just holding hands can strengthen the emotional connection you share. Being physically close with your partner allows you to communicate love and affection without words, reinforcing the bond between you. When you engage in activities that make you both happy, the emotional and physical connection grows, creating a sense of wanting to be around each other more often.

Another important aspect of emotional bonding is trust. Trust isn't just about fidelity—it's about reliability, honesty, and follow-through in all areas of the relationship. Anytime you break a promise, manipulate a situation, or disappoint your partner carelessly, it chips away at the trust you've built. Rebuilding trust is a process that takes time, but it's vital to a healthy relationship. It's worth the effort to restore trust because the security that comes from knowing you can rely on each other is irreplaceable.

If you find that trust in your relationship has been damaged, the first step toward rebuilding it is to be intentional and apologetic. A heartfelt apology, combined with genuine remorse, shows your partner that you're serious about mending the relationship.

Clear and honest communication is also crucial—holding back important details will only hinder the healing process. Your partner needs to fully understand what happened and why in order to move forward.

It's also essential to give your partner the time they need to heal. Rebuilding trust can't be rushed, and the betrayed party deserves all the time they require to process what happened and recover emotionally. Rushing them to move past it too quickly will only stall the healing process.

When trust has been broken, it's tempting to make quick decisions in the heat of the moment. However, it's usually best to take things slowly. Major decisions, like ending the relationship, should be made with careful thought, not out of immediate pain. Reflect on the situation thoroughly before choosing a path forward.

Taking responsibility is another key part of trust rebuilding. The person who caused the hurt must own up to their actions, without getting defensive or making excuses. Accountability is the first step toward making meaningful changes and showing a willingness to rebuild trust.

At the same time, the betrayed partner must learn to let go of the past once trust begins to rebuild. Dwelling on old mistakes will prevent healing. If you see that your partner is making genuine efforts to change and repair the relationship, recognize those efforts and support them by focusing on the progress being made.

Finally, forgiveness is a process that takes time. There's no need to rush it. Gradual forgiveness involves acknowledging the positive steps your partner is taking, rather than expecting immediate perfection. Allow space for improvement, and give your partner the opportunity to rebuild the relationship without frustration or resentment clouding the process.

Simple Action Plan for Strengthening Emotional Bonds

Use the insights gained from the self-assessment and journaling prompts to create an action plan. Focus on one or two areas where you feel improvement is needed, and write down specific actions you and your partner can take to enhance your emotional bond. Here are some example steps to get you started:

1. **Set aside 15 minutes each day for uninterrupted conversation.** Share something meaningful about your day or discuss a deeper topic, without distractions.

2. **Plan a weekly date night or activity that you both enjoy.** Whether it's cooking together, going for a walk, or trying something new, make time for fun and connection.

3. **Practice active listening.** The next time your partner shares something, focus entirely on them. Reflect back what you hear and show empathy without immediately offering advice or solutions.

The 5 Love Languages

Dr. Gary Chapman popularized the concept of love language after realizing that one of the major reasons why couples struggle is the failure to understand each other's needs. As different people, receiving and giving love resonates differently with us. Exploring love despite these differences may require that you and your decrypt each other's love languages.

Love language can be anything, from everyday words of affirmation to emotional support, thoughtful gifts, and physical touch. Each individual can explore different ways of being loved to select the ones that resonate deeply with them. For instance, if you are in love with someone whose love language is receiving gifts, you need to put effort into preparing thoughtful gifts for them. Surprising them with things you know they will appreciate on good or bad days is also an excellent way to communicate love with them.

When two people understand each other's love language in a relationship, it becomes easy to make the right effort and get the best result. At this point, you and your partner are not doing things as you please; instead, you are paying attention to what makes each other feel loved and cherished.

Love language can be used to resolve disputes and offer reassurance and calmness. When your partner communicates their feelings or fears to you, you can decide to do something they love to cheer them up or make them feel better. During illness, spending quality time with someone whose love language is ordinarily spending time with those they love can offer them strength, and it can help them through the physical and emotional pain of being ill.

In his work, Gary proposed 5 notable languages that couples can explore to strengthen their emotional bond and connection, and they are:

Words of affirmation: While everyone needs to hear words of affirmation to keep them going, if positive words are your partner's primary love language, then expressing your love to them through praise and encouragement makes them feel uniquely loved.

Act of service: Those who have struggled with asking for help may find the act of service a way of showing love. Hence, doing the little things that require going out of your way to make them feel good is much appreciated.

Physical touch: Someone whose love language is physical touch will appreciate physical closeness with their partner. Activities like cuddling, holding hands, or even a massage make them feel loved and cherished.

Quality time: If your love language is spending quality time with those you love, knowing that your partner puts effort into being around and giving you their undivided attention will naturally make your day more beautiful.

Receiving gifts: Everyone will appreciate a gift, but for those whose love language is receiving gifts, preparing gifts for them is beyond a mere act of gesture. This has nothing to do with how expensive a gift is; instead, people of this nature tend to focus more on the thoughtfulness and care that goes into picking out something for them solely to make them feel loved and happy.

Embracing love language allows couples to enrich their love life by creating a mindset that is ready to explore deep emotional safety and intimacy. Doing things that make the other person feel loved and communicating your love language with them can transform how you connect emotionally. Also, being open to adapting to each other's love language allows you and your partner to build a deeper and more compassionate relationship.

Essentially, anyone can have more than one love language; however, if you struggle to find your love language, you should explore the options above to determine what makes you feel especially loved and cherished.

Exploring Each Other's Love Languages

After identifying your love languages, engage in a discussion about what makes each expression of love meaningful. For example, if your partner's primary language is Words of Affirmation, talk about the types of words or phrases that make them feel most appreciated, whether they prefer to receive affirmations in person or through written notes, and if certain compliments resonate more deeply than others. For those who value Quality Time, explore what that looks like for them—whether it's spending uninterrupted time together, engaging in shared activities, or simply being present without distractions.

The same thoughtful exploration applies to the other love languages. For those who feel loved through Acts of Service, discuss specific tasks or gestures that make a difference. Do they feel supported when help is offered without asking, or do they prefer collaboration on household chores? For Receiving Gifts, it's essential to understand whether spontaneous surprises or thoughtful presents on special occasions matter more. If Physical Touch is the key, ask about their preferred forms of affection—whether they appreciate casual gestures like holding hands, or whether touch is particularly meaningful during emotional moments.

Once you've had these conversations, take some time to reflect on what you've learned. How can you integrate this newfound understanding into your daily routine? Perhaps it's offering more frequent affirmations or being mindful about spending focused time together. After a week or two of consciously "speaking" each other's love languages, check in with one another. How did it feel to receive love in the ways you prefer? Are there any adjustments or additional actions that could make these experiences even more fulfilling? By continually reflecting and adjusting, you ensure that both partners feel valued and loved in the ways that resonate most with them.

Love Languages Quiz

Instructions: Answer the following questions individually to discover your primary love language. Choose the option that best represents how you feel loved in your relationship.

1. When your partner does something unexpected for you to show they care, like making your favorite meal or doing a chore, you feel:

    A) Loved and appreciated.

    B) It's nice, but I'd prefer spending quality time together.

    C) Grateful, but it's not as important as hearing kind words.

    D) It's a sweet gesture, but I'd love a thoughtful gift more.

    E) It's okay, but a warm hug would mean more.

2. You feel most connected to your partner when:

    A) They tell you how much they appreciate you.

    B) They spend uninterrupted time with you.

    C) They give you a thoughtful gift.

    D) They help you with tasks that lighten your load.

    E) They hold your hand or give you a comforting embrace.

3. When you think about love, you believe it's best shown through:

    A) Saying kind, supportive words.

    B) Devoting time and attention to each other.

    C) Surprising each other with gifts.

    D) Doing things for one another.

    E) Physical touch and closeness.

4. During special occasions, you most look forward to:

    A) Heartfelt cards or verbal affirmations.

    B) Spending quality time together, just the two of us.

    C) Receiving a meaningful gift.

    D) When my partner helps make the day easier.

    E) Extra physical closeness, like cuddling or holding hands.

5. When you're feeling down, what lifts your spirits the most?

A) Encouraging words from my partner.

B) Spending time together, doing something we both enjoy.

C) Receiving a small, thoughtful gift.

D) Having my partner step in to help with things that are overwhelming.

E) A comforting touch or hug from my partner.

Scoring:

- Mostly A's: Words of Affirmation - You value verbal acknowledgments of love, including frequent "I love you," compliments, and words of appreciation.

- Mostly B's: Quality Time - You feel most loved when your partner gives you their undivided attention, free from distractions.

- Mostly C's: Receiving Gifts - You appreciate receiving thoughtful gifts as a visual symbol of love.

- Mostly D's: Acts of Service - You feel loved when your partner helps you with tasks and chores, alleviating some of your burdens.

- Mostly E's: Physical Touch - Physical affection, such as hugs, kisses, and holding hands, is your primary love language.

PARTENR 1:

PARTENR 2:

Common Barriers to Intimacy

Romantic relationships allow us to explore emotional and physical connections. The importance of this aspect of human life has been universally acknowledged by many; however, while there is a widespread desire to explore intimacy, the truth is it is possible to find it hard. Anyone can experience an intimacy block in their relationship, from married couples to girlfriends and boyfriends, and certain things may get in the way of building a deep and intimate connection.

Usually, this intimacy barrier is triggered by the brain when the mind focuses on past or historical events, leading to disconnection between couples. When triggered, it becomes impossible to enjoy a fulfilling love life. However, experiencing these barriers does not need to be the end of your love journey. Couples can work together to overcome them and build a more resilient love.

Identifying common barriers to intimacy can take the form of retrospection or reflective thought process. As stated earlier, your early experiences contribute to how you perceive life in adulthood, and these experiences can affect how easy it is for you or your partner to build intimacy. Some of the barriers you have to overcome may stem from any of these:

Fear of Vulnerability: If you or your partner is scared of showing your vulnerabilities, exploring emotional and physical intimacy to the fullest is impossible. In a relationship, you will have to let it all out without fear or shame, and for this to happen, you must be willing to trust your partner and be vulnerable around them.

Past Trauma: Past trauma may affect the ability to explore emotional or physical intimacy. For instance, someone dealing with anxiety may be unable to engage in physical intimacy. Similarly, past trauma of different kinds may lead to an outstanding level of distrust, making it impossible to trust your partner or connect with them emotionally.

Fear of Abandonment: For someone who has dealt with abandonment in the past, protecting their heart will seem more important than relying on someone. While they may feel the urge to love someone, exploring love to the fullest may be difficult because they do not want to feel that way again.

Past Betrayal: Betrayal from a past or current relationship can break the chain of emotional connection. While some people may be able to overcome this barrier easily, some may struggle to trust again.

Lack of Commitment: If you or your partner are unsure of each other's commitment to the relationship, building a connection will seem like a waste of time. Uncertainty in this part of your relationship may affect how you treat each other, which may determine the level of intimacy you are willing to explore.

Identifying and Managing Barriers

It's important to first take time to reflect on your own. Complete these journaling prompts on your own to gain insight into your personal thoughts and feelings regarding intimacy barriers. Once you've had time to process your own reflections, schedule a conversation with your partner to share your thoughts. This approach allows you both to explore your feelings privately before coming together to discuss how to overcome these barriers as a team.

Reflect on your past experiences with vulnerability

- Journaling Prompt: What does vulnerability mean to me? Why might I be hesitant to show my true self to my partner?
- Guided Conversation: Can we talk about times when we've struggled to be vulnerable with each other? What would help us feel safer to open up?

Consider how past trauma might be influencing your current relationship

- Journaling Prompt: Are there past experiences or traumas that I haven't fully healed from? How might they be impacting my ability to connect with my partner?
- Guided Conversation: Have you noticed moments where past trauma has affected how we interact? How can we support each other through this?

Explore fears of abandonment

- Journaling Prompt: Am I afraid of being abandoned? How has this fear shown up in my relationship, and how has it affected my ability to connect?
- Guided Conversation: What are some ways we can reassure each other that we are fully committed to this relationship?

Address betrayal and its impact on trust

- Journaling Prompt: Have I experienced betrayal in the past, and how has it shaped my ability to trust? What do I need from my partner to rebuild trust?
- Guided Conversation: Let's talk about any past betrayals we've faced—how do they influence the way we trust each other now? What can we do to rebuild or reinforce trust?

Discuss commitment concerns

- Journaling Prompt: Do I ever feel uncertain about my partner's commitment? How does this affect how I approach intimacy?
- Guided Conversation: Are there moments where either of us feels unsure about our level of commitment? How can we strengthen our commitment to each other moving forward?

Overcoming Intimacy Barriers

No matter what is causing an intimacy barrier in your relationship, there are ways to overcome these obstacles and reconnect with your partner. Keep in mind that there is no one-size-fits-all approach—each relationship is unique. The suggestions below are meant to inspire reflection and conversation. Together, you can choose the ideas that resonate most with where you are in your relationship.

Explore Healing

Healing from past trauma or emotional pain is vital for fostering a fulfilling love life. To rebuild trust and learn to be vulnerable, it's important to let go of the triggers that keep pulling you back into old patterns. Healing is a process that can't be rushed; it requires patience and acceptance. Allow yourself to feel vulnerable and open, trusting that this healing will strengthen your emotional connection with your partner.

Discuss Together: Talk openly about any emotional wounds or traumas that might still be impacting your relationship. How can you both support each other in the healing process? Are there specific steps or actions that would make either of you feel safer as you navigate these challenges?

Build Trust

Trust is the foundation of any healthy relationship, and without it, emotional and physical intimacy can be difficult to achieve. If trust has been broken or is lacking, it's important to make rebuilding it a priority. As discussed earlier, trust-building requires consistent actions, open communication, and time.

Discuss Together: Reflect on areas where trust might need to be rebuilt or strengthened. What does trust look like for each of you? Share your thoughts on how you can both contribute to rebuilding trust, and agree on practical steps that feel doable.

Make Necessary Lifestyle Adjustments

Sometimes, everyday life can create barriers to intimacy without you even realizing it. Busy schedules, poor hygiene, inadequate rest, and poor nutrition can all negatively affect your ability to connect with your partner, both emotionally and physically. Consider making adjustments to ensure that your lifestyle supports your relationship rather than detracts from it.

Discuss Together: Take a look at your daily routines and lifestyle habits. Are there small changes either of you could make to improve your connection? Whether it's dedicating more time for each other or improving self-care, discuss ways to adjust your routines so they don't get in the way of intimacy.

Share Experiences

Creating shared experiences can deepen emotional connection and, in turn, lead to greater physical intimacy. Often, when intimacy is lacking, it may be because there hasn't been enough time or effort dedicated to meaningful connection. Engage in activities that allow you to create lasting memories together, such as a romantic dinner, a trip, or even something simple like a walk. These shared experiences help build a foundation of trust and comfort.

Discuss Together: What activities have made you feel closer in the past? Which experiences bring you joy as a couple? Share your ideas for future experiences that could help you reconnect emotionally. Plan something new that excites both of you and allows for vulnerability and closeness.

Explore New Ways to Connect

Sometimes, intimacy barriers arise because the relationship has fallen into predictable routines. If you and your partner are struggling to connect emotionally or physically, it may be time to explore new ways to build your bond. This could mean experimenting with different forms of physical closeness or trying out new sexual activities to reignite passion.

Discuss Together: Share ideas about new activities or experiences that could help you connect more deeply. Is there something you've both been curious to try but haven't yet? Explore new ways to bond, both emotionally and physically, and talk about what you're both comfortable with.

Daily Gratitude and Emotional Intimacy Journaling

Integrating practices like Daily Gratitude and Emotional Intimacy Journaling into your relationship can significantly enhance your emotional connection. These aren't just one-time activities; they are routines that, when consistently applied, can deepen the bond between you and your partner.

Starting each day with a moment of reflection allows you to focus on something specific that you appreciate about your partner. It could be a small gesture from the day before or simply a quality you admire in them. Expressing this appreciation, whether in person, through a note, or even a quick text, creates a habit of positivity. It's not just about saying "thank you" but about genuinely acknowledging the things that make your partner special to you. Over time, this practice shifts the focus of your relationship toward the positive aspects, helping to build a reservoir of goodwill that can be especially beneficial during challenging times.

In the evenings, taking a few minutes before bed to recap your day with your partner can serve as a gentle reminder of the good in your relationship. This practice helps both of you end the day on a positive note, reinforcing your connection before you rest. It's a simple, yet powerful way to stay connected, even when life gets busy. At the end of each week, reflecting together on how these daily expressions of gratitude have impacted your relationship can provide insights into the growth of your emotional bond and help you to continue nurturing it.

Similarly, keeping an Emotional Intimacy Journal is another practice that fosters deeper understanding and communication. By setting aside regular time to write about your thoughts, feelings, and experiences in the relationship, you create a space for self-reflection that can be incredibly therapeutic. Journaling allows you to process your emotions privately and explore any concerns or positive experiences that you may not have shared yet with your partner.

Once a week, sharing select entries from your journal with your partner can open up new avenues for communication. This practice isn't about revealing every thought you have but about choosing moments of vulnerability to share, which can lead to deeper, more meaningful conversations. It encourages both partners to listen actively and respond with empathy, fostering a safe environment where both of you feel understood and supported.

For those who find it difficult to start journaling or are unsure of what to write about, here are some prompts to get you started.

1. **Reflect on a Recent Positive Experience:** Write about a recent moment in your relationship that made you feel loved or appreciated. What happened? How did it make you feel? Why was this moment meaningful to you?

2. **Explore Your Fears:** Consider a fear or worry you have in your relationship. What is it, and where do you think it comes from? How might sharing this fear with your partner help you address it together?

3. **Describe Your Ideal Day Together:** Imagine a perfect day spent with your partner. What would you do? How would it make you feel? What does this ideal day say about what you value most in your relationship?

4. **Write a Letter of Gratitude:** Even if you don't share it, write a letter to your partner expressing your gratitude for them. Focus on specific things they've done recently that you appreciate, as well as the qualities you love about them.

5. **Reflect on a Challenge You've Overcome Together:** Think about a difficult situation that you and your partner have faced. How did you work through it together? What did you learn about each other in the process? How has it strengthened your bond?

6. **Identify Unspoken Desires:** Are there things you wish you could ask for in your relationship but haven't? Write about what those desires are and why you've hesitated to express them. How do you think your partner would respond if you shared these desires?

7. **Document Your Growth as a Couple:** Reflect on how your relationship has grown over time. What have you learned about each other? How have you both changed? What milestones have been particularly significant for you?

8. **Explore Your Emotional Needs:** What do you need emotionally from your partner to feel secure and loved in your relationship? How well do you feel those needs are being met? What could improve?

9. **Write About a Conflict:** Think about a recent disagreement you had with your partner. How did it start? What emotions were involved? How was it resolved? What would you like to do differently next time?

10. **Dream About the Future:** Where do you see your relationship in five years? Ten years? What are your hopes and dreams for your future together? How can you work together to make those dreams a reality?

Love Maps

In every strong relationship, emotional intimacy is built on knowing your partner deeply. Dr. John Gottman, an expert in relationship psychology, introduced the concept of "Love Maps" to highlight the importance of understanding each other's inner worlds. A Love Map is essentially the detailed knowledge you hold about your partner—knowing their likes, dislikes, dreams, memories, and even their biggest fears. This deeper understanding forms the foundation for emotional connection and empathy, and the exercise is designed to strengthen that bond.

To begin, set aside time together in a quiet and relaxed environment, free from distractions. This exercise thrives when both partners are fully engaged, present, and genuinely curious about each other. The questions you'll ask may seem simple, but they provide valuable insight into your partner's emotional landscape. Start by asking questions like:

- *What are your top three life dreams?*
- *Who has been the most influential person in your life?*
- *What are your biggest worries right now?*
- *What is something you've always wanted to try but haven't yet?*
- *What is one of your favorite memories from our time together?*
- *What are three things that make you feel most loved and appreciated?*
- *What's a difficult experience that shaped who you are today?*
- *What do you think is our biggest strength as a couple?*
- *What is a skill or hobby you've always wanted to develop or improve?*
- *What is your biggest goal for the next year?*

As your partner shares their answers, practice active listening. Tune into their words and the emotions behind them. Show genuine interest by asking follow-up questions or seeking clarification on something they've shared. The goal here is to deepen your understanding, not just of the facts, but of how your partner thinks and feels.

One of the most important aspects of Love Maps is their dynamic nature. People change over time—their dreams evolve, their fears shift, and their preferences may differ from year to year. That's why it's essential to periodically revisit this exercise, updating your Love Map with new insights as your relationship grows and changes. By doing so, you ensure that both of you stay emotionally connected, adapting to each other's evolving inner worlds.

Additional Love Map Questions and Themes:

Childhood and Family

- *What is your favorite childhood memory?*
- *Who was your closest family member growing up, and why?*
- *What was a challenge you faced during your childhood, and how did you overcome it?*

- **Life Dreams and Goals**

- *What are three things you want to achieve in the next five years?*
- *If you could have any job, regardless of money or skills, what would it be and why?*
- *What's one dream you've had since you were a child that you still hold onto today?*

Daily Life and Stressors

- *What is something that has been stressing you out lately?*
- *How do you like to relax after a hard day?*
- *What's something small that would make your day better?*

Values and Beliefs

- *What core values are most important to you in life?*
- *How do you feel about the role of spirituality or religion in your life?*
- *What do you believe is the most important quality in a person?*

Relationship and Love

- *What are three things you think we do well as a couple?*
- *What's one area in our relationship that you'd like to work on?*
- *How do you prefer to be shown love and affection?*

Hobbies and Interests

- *What's a hobby or interest you've always wanted to pursue but haven't yet?*
- *How do you like to spend your free time?*
- *What was the best vacation you ever had, and why?*

Friendships and Social Life

- *Who is your best friend, and what do you value most about that relationship?*
- *How do you feel about the role of socializing in our lives?*
- *What do you think about maintaining friendships outside of our relationship?*

Personal Strengths and Challenges

- *What do you consider your greatest strength?*
- *What's a personal challenge you've been working on?*
- *How can I support you in your personal growth?*

Memories and Significant Events

- *What is the most memorable date we've had together?*
- *What's a significant life event that shaped who you are today?*
- *What's a funny or embarrassing moment we've shared that still makes you laugh?*

Future and Planning

- *Where do you see us living in the future?*
- *How do you feel about starting a family (or expanding our family)?*
- *What's one adventure or experience you'd like us to share together?*

PARTNER 1	
3 LIFE DREAMS	INFLUENCIAL PERSON
BIGGEST WORRIES NOW	YOU ALWAYS WANTED
FAVORITE MEMORY	3 THINGS YOU FEEL LOVED
WHAT SHAPED YOU	OUR BIGGEST STRENGTH
HOBBIE	GOAL FOR NEXT YEAR

PARTNER 2	
3 LIFE DREAMS	INFLUENCIAL PERSON
BIGGEST WORRIES NOW	YOU ALWAYS WANTED
FAVORITE MEMORY	3 THINGS YOU FEEL LOVED
WHAT SHAPED YOU	OUR BIGGEST STRENGTH
HOBBIE	GOAL FOR NEXT YEAR

Week 6

Balancing Life and Relationship

Whether it's dealing with personal family issues or managing work, there are likely times when life has interfered with your relationship. If you're particularly passionate about your work, you may find it challenging to balance both work and your relationship. Imagine having a rough day at the office—you're preparing for an important presentation, but the slides just won't come together. While juggling this task, your partner may be trying to reach you about something urgent, yet you feel you can't spare a minute.

Moments like these can quickly escalate, leaving your partner feeling like you prioritize work over the relationship. You might soon realize two things: First, your work and personal life exist in separate spheres that demand your attention. Second, despite the importance of your job, your relationship also deserves care and focus.

Until you find a balance between your relationship and other responsibilities, this kind of conflict may continue. You may frequently wake up with the unsettling question of what truly deserves more of your time and energy.

Finding balance isn't just important—it's inevitable if you want a fulfilling life and a thriving relationship. Every couple must find ways to ensure that the demands of daily life don't stifle the growth of their relationship. At the same time, it's crucial that the relationship doesn't obstruct personal passions or professional pursuits.

To enjoy a fulfilling relationship, you need to live a fulfilling life. Many couples have reported that maintaining a busy schedule can actually have positive effects on their relationship. For some, it reduces the likelihood of unnecessary arguments, while for others, having a well-rounded partner who is passionate about their own interests brings a unique and healthy dynamic to the relationship.

Striking a balance between your personal responsibilities and your relationship offers benefits to both you and your partner. When you invest in your own well-being and maintain a balanced life, you contribute to the overall quality of the relationship. Over-committing to work, for example, can negatively affect not only your personal life but your professional life as well. On the other hand, creating balance allows you to rest, recharge, and gain fresh perspectives—enhancing all areas of your life.

While it's important to prioritize your love life, other aspects of your life deserve attention too. With the right strategies, balancing these priorities doesn't have to mean sacrificing one for the other.

––––––––

A healthy relationship thrives in an environment where both partners prioritize spending quality time together and being emotionally present. Achieving balance becomes easier when both partners are committed to understanding and supporting each other, even during busy or stressful times.

Stress Management

Stress is an inevitable part of life, and how we manage it often defines the quality of our daily experiences. However, rather than seeing stress as something purely negative, it's important to recognize that it can sometimes lead to personal growth. For instance, starting a new job can feel overwhelming, but it also offers opportunities to meet new people, gain knowledge, and find a more fulfilling environment. The key is in how we choose to respond to these situations and the strategies we use to manage stress effectively.

A significant part of stress management is tied to self-care—the practice of looking after your mental, emotional, and physical well-being. Self-care isn't just a personal endeavor but an essential part of building a healthy relationship, as both you and your partner need to support each other while also prioritizing your individual needs. To truly thrive as a couple, it's important to explore self-care strategies alongside stress management techniques, ensuring that both your relationship and personal peace are protected.

Identify Your Personal Needs

Self-care begins with understanding what you need to feel balanced and fulfilled. This involves identifying the things that replenish your energy and help you feel at ease, whether that's engaging in hobbies, reading books to enhance your mental and intellectual growth, or staying active through regular exercise. By being intentional about your needs, you create the foundation for a more resilient and stress-free life. Stress management, in turn, becomes easier when you're fulfilling these personal needs, as they help you recharge and face challenges with more clarity and focus.

Explore Your Interests

Once you've identified your needs, don't hesitate to prioritize them. Make time for the things that bring you joy and help you grow. Whether it's finding time to meditate, taking long walks, or spending an afternoon on a hobby you love, integrating these activities into your routine becomes a form of proactive stress relief. By nourishing yourself in this way, you're also better equipped to manage stress when it arises, because you've built a solid base of well-being and balance.

Balance Work and Life

Work-life balance is another crucial part of both stress management and self-care. Often, the stress we experience comes from feeling overwhelmed by work obligations that spill over into our personal lives. Setting clear boundaries for your work hours can help alleviate this. When you allocate specific times for work and commit to sticking to them, you free up energy and time to focus on other important aspects of your life, like spending quality time with your partner or engaging in self-care routines. This balance prevents burnout and allows you to recharge, improving not just your work life but your personal relationships as well.

Control Your Body's Reaction

Managing stress requires learning how to control your body's natural response to external situations. Stress often arises not from the situation itself but from how we interpret and react to it. For instance, if your car breaks down and you have to walk unexpectedly, your initial reaction may be one of frustration or stress. But by reframing your mindset—perhaps seeing the walk as an opportunity for exercise or a chance to slow down—you can reduce that stress. How you respond shapes the experience, and learning to adjust your perspective can help make stressful moments more manageable.

Understanding Yourself and Setting Priorities

Just as you need to identify your personal needs for self-care, understanding your stress triggers is equally vital. People experience stress differently, and what might be overwhelming for one person may not be for another. By recognizing your specific triggers, you can begin to develop tailored strategies for managing stress. This self-awareness helps you focus on solutions that are truly effective for you, whether it's avoiding unnecessary stressors or preparing for challenging situations ahead of time.

Alongside this, setting priorities is crucial for stress management. Life can feel overwhelming when you're juggling multiple responsibilities. Instead of tackling everything at once, break your tasks into manageable chunks. Create a to-do list, focusing on one thing at a time, and prioritize tasks based on urgency and importance. This approach not only eases stress but also gives you a greater sense of control over your life.

Taking Time Off and Adjusting Expectations

Incorporating regular breaks into your routine is essential for self-care and managing stress. Whether it's a short walk, reading a book, or watching a movie, stepping away from your tasks allows you to relax and reset. These breaks are crucial for recharging your energy, so you can return to your tasks with a fresh mind and renewed focus.

At the same time, it's important to keep your expectations realistic. While it's great to have high aspirations, unrealistic goals can create unnecessary stress. Recognizing that perfection isn't always attainable allows you to manage your efforts without feeling overwhelmed. Growth takes time, and by setting achievable goals, you can reduce stress and focus on meaningful progress.

Preparing for Change and Prioritizing Health

Another way to manage stress effectively is by preparing for change. Change is inevitable, and learning how to adapt to it can significantly reduce stress. By practicing how to handle transitions and new situations, you build resilience, making it easier to navigate challenges. Embracing change as a natural part of life helps you feel more grounded and less overwhelmed when it arises.

———

Finally, prioritizing your physical health plays a crucial role in managing stress. Staying active, eating well, and maintaining a healthy lifestyle equip you to handle stress more effectively. Physical well-being gives you the energy and mental clarity needed to cope with daily challenges. For example, if you're physically fit, even unexpected tasks like walking a long distance can feel more like an opportunity for exercise than an inconvenience.

Relaxation Techniques

Relaxation techniques are essential tools for managing stress and maintaining emotional balance. These techniques can help you calm your mind, reduce physical tension, and regain a sense of control during stressful times. By incorporating relaxation practices into your daily routine, you can create a more peaceful and centered approach to life.

Deep Breathing Exercises: Focus on taking slow, deep breaths to calm the nervous system. Inhale deeply through your nose, hold the breath for a few seconds, and then exhale slowly through your mouth. Repeat for several minutes.

Progressive Muscle Relaxation: Tense each muscle group in your body, starting from your toes and working up to your head. Hold the tension for a few seconds, then slowly release it, noticing the sensation of relaxation that follows.

Mindfulness Meditation: Sit quietly and focus on your breath or a mantra. Allow thoughts to pass without judgment, returning your focus to your breathing whenever your mind wanders.

Guided Imagery: Visualize a peaceful scene or situation. Use all your senses to imagine the sights, sounds, and feelings of this place, allowing yourself to relax into the imagery.

Morning Practice: Start your day with a few minutes of deep breathing or mindfulness meditation to set a calm tone for the day.

Evening Wind-Down: Use progressive muscle relaxation or guided imagery before bed to release the day's stress and prepare for restful sleep.

Shared Relaxation: Engage in these techniques with your partner to reduce stress together and strengthen your emotional bond. This shared experience can enhance your connection and provide mutual support.

Time Management Strategies for Couples

Managing time as a couple can feel like a delicate dance—each partner may have their own rhythm, working in different fields, following different interests, and juggling separate schedules. However, for a relationship to truly thrive, it's important to find ways to harmonize these differences. By employing effective time management strategies, you and your partner can ensure that, despite the demands of everyday life, your relationship remains a priority.

The goal isn't to wake up one day and realize your lives have drifted too far apart. Instead, by being intentional about your time, you can create a shared plan that helps both of you meet in the middle. Time management strategies ensure that you're not just surviving your relationship amid life's busyness but actively working toward a better, more connected partnership. By aligning your schedules and making time for shared goals, you and your partner can stay on the same page.

Working Towards Big Goals

One of the most effective ways to align your time management as a couple is by working together toward larger goals. These goals might be long-term aspirations, such as buying a house, starting a family, or planning for major life changes. But to work effectively as a team, you need a shared understanding of what you're working toward.

A helpful strategy is to hold a vision session, where you and your partner sit down together to discuss your shared goals and dreams. Think of it as running a successful organization—both partners need to contribute ideas and discuss the best path forward. In this session, you can discuss your larger aspirations, like saving for a home or planning for a big vacation, and ensure you're both on the same page about what you're working toward.

Once your goals are clear, you can create a roadmap for achieving them. Life doesn't revolve solely around your relationship, so it's essential to consider your individual responsibilities and demands as well. A detailed plan, complete with timelines and specific responsibilities for each partner, ensures that you're consistently making progress toward your shared goals while still managing your day-to-day lives. This kind of structure keeps you both focused and helps avoid confusion or misalignment.

Managing Chores as a Team

Chores may not seem like a big deal at first, but over time, they can become a source of stress or imbalance in a relationship if not handled equitably. One way to manage this is by setting aside specific times for handling household tasks together. Instead of tackling chores as they arise, you can schedule regular times to get things done, whether it's cleaning the house, doing laundry, or tackling yard work. By sharing these responsibilities, you ensure that neither partner feels overwhelmed or burdened.

You can also make chores more manageable by creating an inventory of tasks. This allows you to keep track of what needs to be done and decide together how to prioritize these chores. If one partner is always in charge of certain tasks, consider rotating responsibilities so no one gets stuck with the same routine and boredom doesn't set in. Rotating chores also ensures that both partners understand the effort required to keep things running smoothly at home.

Making Time for Each Other

Amid the hustle of work, family obligations, and social commitments, it's easy to let quality time with your partner slip through the cracks. But spending meaningful time together is essential for maintaining a strong connection. One strategy to manage this is time blocking—setting aside specific blocks of time in your schedule dedicated solely to your partner. Whether it's 30-60 minutes before bed to unwind together or planning fun weekend activities, intentionally making time for each other ensures that your relationship remains a priority.

Another helpful practice is creating gadget-free zones during your quality time together. In our tech-driven world, it's all too easy to be distracted by notifications, emails, or social media. But these interruptions can prevent meaningful conversations and genuine connection. By designating specific times or places where phones, tablets, and computers aren't allowed, you can ensure that when you're together, your attention is fully on each other.

Stress Inventory

This exercise helps you identify the specific situations, environments, or behaviors that contribute to your stress levels. By pinpointing these stressors, you can begin to develop strategies to address them and reduce their impact on your well-being and relationship.

Start by setting aside some quiet time to reflect on your daily life. Think about the moments or situations that consistently make you feel stressed. This could be anything from work-related pressures to personal challenges or even recurring conflicts in your relationship. As you reflect, write down each stressor in your Stress Inventory.

PARTNER 1		PARTNER 2	
STRESSOR	FREQUENCY	STRESSOR	FREQUENCY

Next, consider the frequency and intensity of each stressor. Are these situations daily occurrences, or do they happen only occasionally? How severe is the stress they cause? By categorizing your stressors in this way, you can begin to see patterns in your stress levels and identify the most significant contributors.

Once you've completed your inventory, discuss your findings with your partner. Sharing your stress inventory can help your partner understand what you're going through and foster empathy and support in your relationship. Together, you can brainstorm ways to reduce or manage these stressors, whether that involves making changes in your routine, setting boundaries, or finding new coping mechanisms.

Time Management Plan

Poor time management is a common source of stress, often leading to feelings of overwhelm and frustration. Creating a Time Management Plan helps you organize your day, prioritize tasks, and ensure that you have time for both responsibilities and relaxation.

Start by listing all the tasks and responsibilities you need to manage daily, both at work and in your personal life. Include everything—from meetings and work deadlines to household chores and time with your partner. Once you have a comprehensive list, prioritize these tasks based on their urgency and importance.

Next, create a daily or weekly schedule that allocates specific times for each task. Be realistic about how long each activity will take, and build in breaks to avoid burnout. It's also important to schedule time for relaxation and activities that bring you joy, such as hobbies, exercise, or spending quality time with your partner.

As you implement your Time Management Plan, be flexible and open to adjustments. Life is unpredictable, and sometimes things won't go according to plan. If this happens, re-evaluate your schedule and adjust your priorities as needed. The goal is not to create a rigid timetable but to establish a structure that helps you manage your time more effectively.

Discuss your Time Management Plan with your partner, especially if you share responsibilities or have joint activities. This ensures that both of you are on the same page and can support each other in maintaining a balanced routine.

Week 7

Long-Term Relationship Goals

Throughout your relationship, you will reach many checkpoints—times when you can reflect on what went wrong, highlight factors affecting the growth of your relationship, and ponder the next course of action. At those moments, you have the chance to make new choices and shift the trajectory of your relationship. You can decide to move forward with plans and goals that align with your desired future, or you can throw together haphazard ideas, abandon them, and repeat the same experiences.

The ultimate long-term goal for every healthy and beautiful relationship is to build a life together. When you come across a video of two people still deeply in love after many years, your heart might say, "This is what I want, too." However, when it comes to the question of what keeps two people together for the long run, research shows a wide range of answers. This leads us to understand that questions like "What's the secret to a lasting marriage?" or "How do I ensure my partner stays with me forever?" can't be answered definitively. Even if you were to mimic the lifestyle of a happy couple today, you might not get the same results.

Resilient and lasting love stories require ongoing effort and commitment. What will keep you and your partner going is more than the initial attraction that drew you together. While passion and chemistry may have ignited the relationship, it is shared purpose and long-term vision that sustain it over time. Achieving this requires both partners to be proactive in setting and working towards long-term goals.

One of the core ingredients of a lasting relationship is shared vision. When you and your partner have a common direction—whether it's building a family, advancing your careers, or creating a shared lifestyle—you lay the foundation for growth. Setting these shared goals ensures that both of you are actively participating in shaping your future together. These goals could range from smaller, immediate ones, like saving for a vacation, to bigger ones, like buying a home or planning retirement. The key is to regularly revisit and revise them to reflect where you both are in life, ensuring you remain aligned as a couple.

Another vital element is trust and transparency. Building long-term trust requires clarity about your values, intentions, and plans as a couple. When you and your partner commit to being transparent about what you want from the relationship and actively work toward those shared goals, it fosters a deeper level of intimacy and confidence in the future. Without this, the relationship risks stagnation, as unresolved doubts can cause cracks in your foundation.

Adaptability is also essential. Life rarely goes exactly according to plan, and neither will your relationship. The ability to adapt to changes—whether they be external circumstances like job changes or internal shifts like evolving emotional needs—will define the longevity of your partnership. Couples who set long-term goals but are also flexible in adjusting them when life throws curveballs tend to build stronger, more resilient bonds. Instead of rigidly sticking to a plan that no longer serves you, you learn to navigate the ebbs and flows of life together, adjusting your course as necessary.

A lasting relationship thrives on commitment to growth, not only as a couple but as individuals. Setting long-term goals requires both partners to be open to personal growth and continuous self-improvement. Supporting each other's ambitions and giving each other the space to evolve individually is crucial. For example, you may set goals around personal development, like supporting each other through career changes, educational pursuits, or exploring new interests. This individual growth can feed into your relationship, making it more dynamic and exciting.

One of the most understated ingredients of long-term relationships is playfulness and joy. While goals and responsibilities are important, lasting couples don't forget to have fun together. They celebrate the small wins, share inside jokes, and maintain a sense of playfulness that keeps the relationship light and enjoyable. As you set long-term goals, it's essential to prioritize joy and adventure. Make sure that the vision you create for your future also includes time for spontaneity, laughter, and shared experiences that remind you why you're together in the first place.

Additionally, consistency is what bridges short-term actions and long-term success. Small, consistent acts of love and support, like showing appreciation, spending quality time together, or actively listening, contribute to the longevity of the relationship. Achieving your long-term goals as a couple is less about grand gestures and more about these daily, intentional choices to nurture the relationship.

Lastly, patience and perseverance are crucial in any long-term relationship. The goals you set together may not always come easily. Life's challenges—whether financial setbacks, personal struggles, or unexpected detours—will test the strength of your bond. However, couples who are patient with each other, who are willing to work through setbacks instead of giving up, tend to come out stronger. This patience isn't passive; it's an active choice to keep building, even when the journey is tough.

As you and your partner set long-term goals, it's important to remember that these key ingredients—shared vision, trust, adaptability, commitment to growth, playfulness, consistency, and patience—are what help relationships thrive. These elements serve as guideposts as you move forward together, ensuring that the life you're building isn't just about reaching milestones but about creating a meaningful, enduring connection.

Setting and Achieving Long-Term Goals

The decision to make better plans for you and your partner is a significant first step, but seeing those plans through requires more than just that initial decision. If you're someone who's already goal-oriented, you know that once the excitement fades, you need a clear strategy to move forward. However, if goal-setting feels unfamiliar or overwhelming, don't worry—this part is for you.

It's normal to feel a rush of enthusiasm when you first think about setting goals, but the real work begins when that excitement starts to wear off. The key to making lasting changes in your relationship isn't just hoping things will improve; it's about having a solid plan. With the right approach, even if you're not naturally inclined to set goals, you can learn how to work toward something meaningful.

Long-term relationships are built on mutual respect, equality, understanding, and consistent effort from both partners. It's not about one person carrying the weight—it's about working together. Whether one partner initiates a goal or both come to it together, the important thing is that you collaborate and stay committed to making it happen.

The good news is that our brains are wired to respond to meaningful goals. When you set long-term goals that are exciting and important, it naturally motivates you to take action. Even fun activities, like planning a trip together or making time for shared hobbies, can become long-term goals that strengthen your bond. Don't shy away from adding joy to your goals—it's just as important as the serious ones!

However, it's also normal for that initial burst of excitement to wear off, especially when life gets in the way. When you notice this happening, it's an opportunity to take action and reignite the energy that first brought you to create those goals in the first place.

One helpful approach is to periodically check in and reassess your goals. Take time to revisit what you've set out to achieve and reflect on the progress you've made so far. Remember, progress isn't always linear—sometimes it may feel slow or stagnant, but reflecting on the strides you've already taken can boost your motivation. This is also a good time to discuss with your partner whether the goals still align with both of your visions. As time goes on, desires or circumstances might shift, so it's perfectly fine to adjust or tweak your goals to better suit your current needs.

If the goals you're working towards start to feel overwhelming, breaking them down into smaller, more manageable steps can make a significant difference. Large goals can seem intimidating, but achieving smaller milestones along the way helps maintain momentum. Each small accomplishment brings with it a renewed sense of purpose, making the overall journey feel more achievable.

Another essential element to keep the energy alive is to celebrate the small wins. Don't wait until the end to acknowledge your progress—every milestone is worth recognition. These celebrations don't have to be grand gestures. Sometimes a simple dinner, a special activity, or even a moment of reflection together is enough to remind you of how far you've come. Celebrating along the way keeps the journey fun and reinforces the connection between you and your partner.

In moments when motivation fades, lean on each other for support. If one of you is feeling discouraged, the other can provide encouragement. Relationships are a partnership, and sometimes all it takes is a gentle reminder of why you're working towards these goals together. That shared support can be the key to reigniting your enthusiasm.

Lastly, if the goal starts to feel more like a chore than something exciting, try reframing it. Focus on the benefits you'll experience once you achieve it. For example, instead of viewing a goal like saving for a house as a financial burden, shift your perspective to envision the home you'll create together and the memories you'll build in that space. Reframing helps transform a daunting task into something meaningful, reminding you both why it matters and how it will enhance your life together.

Identifying Your Goals

When identifying goals in your relationship, it's crucial to remember that personal and shared aspirations can span a wide range. From everyday concerns like dividing household chores to long-term dreams such as buying a house or raising a family, the goals you set together shape your path forward. While it's easy to get caught up in the big picture—like building your life together—achieving those larger ambitions is often a matter of breaking them down into smaller, more manageable steps.

For example, if you've noticed that you've been feeling emotionally or physically disconnected, you might set a goal to improve intimacy. Other goals could focus on balancing different parenting styles, working towards financial stability, or simply supporting one another in individual pursuits like career development or personal hobbies.

There are different types of goals you can set, depending on what you want to achieve as a couple. For example, problem-solving goals help turn challenges into opportunities for growth, like organizing household responsibilities if they've become a source of tension. Family goals revolve around key decisions such as marriage, having children, or establishing shared parenting styles, which strengthen the foundation of your relationship.

Financial goals play a significant role in maintaining stability, allowing you to align on budgeting, saving, and long-term investments to secure your future together. In addition to these practical goals, you can focus on emotional and physical connection goals—enhancing communication or reigniting intimacy to strengthen your bond.

It's also crucial to prioritize personal development goals, supporting each other's individual growth, whether advancing in your career, learning new skills, or nurturing a creative passion. Your personal goals are integral to the success of the relationship.

Health and wellness goals are another essential aspect, as maintaining physical and mental well-being positively impacts both partners. Setting goals around fitness, stress management, or nutrition ensures that both of you feel your best, which naturally supports the relationship. Finally, travel goals—whether a weekend getaway or a larger vacation—allow you to create shared experiences and deepen your connection by exploring new places together.

The process starts with a shared vision. Talk with your partner about what you both want in your relationship and map out specific goals to help you get there. These goals don't have to feel overwhelming; they can range from dedicating more time to each other weekly to planning long-term financial strategies, such as saving for a home or retirement.

One technique that can help make this process more structured and achievable is the SMART goal-setting method. The SMART framework stands for Specific, Measurable, Attainable, Relevant, and Time-bound—criteria that ensure your goals are clear, actionable, and realistic. For instance, if your goal is to improve your financial situation, break it down using the SMART criteria:

- **Specific:** Set a clear goal like cutting monthly expenses, reducing discretionary spending, or investing savings.
- **Measurable:** Aim to save a specific amount, like $60,000 over a year by contributing $5,000 monthly to savings.
- **Attainable:** Make sure your goal is realistic given your current financial circumstances.
- **Relevant:** Align the goal with your shared long-term plans, like saving for a home or retirement.
- **Time-bound**: Set a timeframe, such as achieving the goal within 12 months, with check-ins along the way.

The importance of a Timeframe

Once you've identified your goals, setting a realistic timeframe is crucial. Without a clear timeframe, a goal becomes more of a vague aspiration than something tangible to work towards. Timeframes provide structure and a sense of urgency, helping to keep both partners accountable and focused on the progress. They prevent burnout by giving you clear milestones and moments to reflect on how far you've come.

Relationship goals can vary greatly in their scope and duration. For example, you might have a short-term goal, like improving communication within the next week by trying a specific technique such as active listening during conversations. On the other hand, long-term goals, like saving for a house or planning for retirement, can stretch over several years. Both types of goals are equally important, and you don't have to limit yourself to working on just one at a time. You can, for example, tackle a big goal like saving for a house while also focusing on smaller, more immediate goals like improving your daily routines or carving out quality time for each other.

It's also important to check in regularly, ideally weekly, to evaluate how well you're sticking to your plan. Are you making progress, or do you need to readjust? These regular check-ins create opportunities to celebrate the small victories and rework the approach if necessary. This habit will reinforce the feeling that you're playing on the same team, actively working together toward shared goals. It builds accountability and helps you both stay connected, as each partner is invested in keeping things on track. Not only does this create a more productive approach to goal-setting, but it also strengthens your relationship by fostering teamwork and mutual support.

Vision Board Creation

Creating a vision board together is a powerful way for couples to visualize and solidify their shared dreams and aspirations. This exercise allows you to explore and define what you both want for your future, making your goals more tangible and aligned.

Start by gathering materials for your vision board: magazines, scissors, glue, markers, and a large board or poster. Spend some time individually thinking about your dreams and goals for your relationship, then come together to share your thoughts.

Begin by cutting out images, words, and phrases that resonate with your vision for the future. These could represent anything from travel destinations, financial goals, family aspirations, or the kind of home you envision. As you work together, discuss why each element is important to you and how it reflects your shared values.

Once you've collected enough material, arrange and glue them onto the board in a way that feels meaningful to both of you. Place the vision board somewhere visible in your home, where it can serve as a daily reminder of your shared goals and the future you're working towards together.

Goal-Setting Exercise

This exercise helps you define specific, actionable goals that align with your shared vision and values, providing a roadmap for your future together.

Begin by discussing the key areas of your relationship where you'd like to set goals. This could include areas such as financial planning, career aspirations, family planning, health and wellness, or personal growth.

For each area, brainstorm specific goals you want to achieve as a couple. Make sure these goals are SMART (Specific, Measurable, Achievable, Relevant, and Time-bound). For example, instead of saying, "We want to save money," set a specific goal like, "We will save $10,000 over the next 12 months by reducing our spending on non-essentials."

Once you've established your goals, write them down and create an action plan. This plan should outline the steps you'll take to achieve each goal, assign responsibilities, and set timelines for when you'll check in on your progress.

INTIMICY & ROMANCE

Specific:

Measurable:

Achivable:

Relevant:

Time-bound:

FINANCIAL PLANNING

Specific:

Measurable:

Achivable:

Relevant:

Time-bound:

FAMILY PLANNING

Specific:

Measurable:

Achivable:

Relevant:

Time-bound:

CAREER ASPIRATIONS - PARTNER 1

Specific:

Measurable:

Achivable:

Relevant:

Time-bound:

HEALTH & WELLNESS - PARTNER 1

Specific:

Measurable:

Achivable:

Relevant:

Time-bound:

PERSONAL GROWTH - PARTNER 1

Specific:

Measurable:

Achivable:

Relevant:

Time-bound:

CAREER ASPIRATIONS - PARTNER 2

Specific:

Measurable:

Achivable:

Relevant:

Time-bound:

HEALTH & WELLNESS - PARTNER 2

Specific:

Measurable:

Achivable:

Relevant:

Time-bound:

PERSONAL GROWTH - PARTNER 2

Specific:

Measurable:

Achivable:

Relevant:

Time-bound:

Extra

Parenting and Family Dynamics

I grew up in an emotionally unstable family where affection was scarce and arguments were frequent. My parents didn't show much love for each other—or for us—at least not in a way we could recognize. The tension in the house was palpable most days. There was always something simmering just below the surface, ready to erupt. My parents often fought about things that seemed insignificant, and it wasn't uncommon for days to pass in silence after an argument. As a child, I found myself walking on eggshells, never quite sure when the next conflict would arise.

The absence of affection was perhaps even more telling. Hugs and loving words were a rarity, and physical expressions of care were nearly nonexistent. It wasn't that they didn't love us—at least, I believe they did—but they didn't know how to show it. And as a child, you don't always understand that. You only feel the coldness and the disconnection. I internalized a lot of that emotional tension, and as I grew older, it began to shape how I viewed relationships and intimacy.

For a long time, I struggled with showing affection and being vulnerable with others. I feared that showing love or expressing my emotions would make me weak or expose me to rejection. Serious relationships felt like enormous commitments that I wasn't sure I could handle. The emotional baggage I carried from my childhood seeped into every romantic connection I tried to build. I had walls up, and I couldn't easily let anyone in.

It wasn't until I made the decision to work on myself and confront those deeply ingrained patterns that I began to heal. It was a process—one that involved therapy, self-reflection, and a lot of hard work. I had to unlearn the unhealthy dynamics I had witnessed growing up and relearn how to give and receive love in a healthy, constructive way. I learned that affection and vulnerability are not signs of weakness but of strength, and that conflict, when handled with care, can deepen a connection rather than destroy it.

Now, in my own relationships, I make a conscious effort to show affection, communicate openly, and resolve conflicts in a way that is respectful and loving. It hasn't been easy, but I've seen the difference it makes not only in my own life but in how I connect with others. I know from experience that when children grow up in a home without affection or healthy conflict resolution, it can create emotional barriers that are hard to break down as adults. But with intentional effort, those patterns can be changed.

While parenting is traditionally viewed as raising children, it's also essential to consider how the dynamics within your relationship as a couple impact the overall family structure. The health of your relationship creates a foundation for family dynamics, and this dynamic, in turn, shapes your children's emotional and social development. Your ability to manage differences, resolve conflicts, and show affection directly affects how your children perceive love, communication, and resilience.

Family dynamics are not just about shared values; they also represent the ability of your family to adapt and grow. As you and your partner develop as individuals and as a couple, your family grows with you. The values you impart to your children are shaped by how you navigate life's challenges together. When your children observe you making decisions, compromising, or offering each other emotional support, they learn not only about family but about what a healthy relationship looks like.

As parents, your interactions with each other—whether loving, supportive, or strained—leave lasting impressions on your children. When you show mutual respect and admiration for each other, your children will begin to model these behaviors in their interactions. If your partnership lacks open communication or is riddled with unresolved conflict, your children are more likely to absorb these patterns as well.

The importance of learning how to manage conflict and show affection in a healthy manner cannot be overstated. When conflicts are managed constructively, and affection is expressed freely, children develop emotional stability and healthy coping mechanisms. On the other hand, when conflict is unmanaged or affection is absent, children may struggle with their own emotional regulation, experience anxiety, or have difficulty forming healthy relationships in the future.

Parenting is one of the most rewarding and fulfilling roles in life. As your little one holds your hand and looks up to you for guidance, something within you knows you've got to do a good job. The impact of your relationship on your children cannot be overestimated; this is because children learn everything from their parents. From everyday interaction to how you cherish and support each other, your children internalize these traits, and gradually, they become a cornerstone of their value system.

A positive and supportive family is an environment where vibrant and confident children are raised. Providing children with emotional stability ensures they grow into adults who appreciate safety and value communication. Conversely, raising children in an unstable family can impact them negatively.

As parents, you are role models. When children see how you manage stress, resolve conflicts, and show love, they mimic these behaviors as they grow. Conflict resolution is a key skill they will learn by watching how you handle disagreements. A family where conflict is resolved with respect teaches children to value compromise and empathy. In contrast, witnessing constant unresolved tension or arguments without resolution can create insecurities or lead to avoidance of conflict in their adult lives.

Parenting isn't just a role; it's a partnership. Even when one partner is more available than the other, teamwork is crucial. When couples work together, they provide their children with a stable environment where love, support, and growth thrive.

Common Parenting Styles

Balancing your relationship and daily life is already challenging enough, but when parenting is added to the equation, things can become even more complicated. While every parent brings their unique personality and values to raising children, understanding the different parenting styles and their impact can help create a balanced, nurturing environment for your child. Each style has its own strengths and weaknesses, and finding the right balance involves blending these approaches to suit your family's needs. Let's explore the four main parenting styles individually and then look at how you can combine them to create a more balanced and harmonious family dynamic.

Authoritative Style: The authoritative style is often seen as the most balanced and effective because it combines high expectations with emotional support. Parents using this approach set clear rules and boundaries for their children, but they also take the time to explain the reasoning behind those rules. They are responsive to their children's needs and are open to communication. This helps children develop a strong sense of self-discipline, responsibility, and emotional security.

The advantage of this style is that children raised in authoritative households often feel supported and understood, while still learning the importance of rules and structure. However, the challenge for parents is maintaining that delicate balance between being firm and being empathetic. It can be easy to become too lenient or, on the other hand, too rigid in enforcing rules.

Authoritarian Style: In contrast to the authoritative approach, authoritarian parenting is more focused on control and discipline. Parents who use this style set strict rules and expect obedience without much room for discussion or emotional support. While this approach can help instill a sense of order and respect for authority, it often comes at the cost of emotional connection.

Children raised in authoritarian households may struggle with self-esteem or have difficulty making independent decisions because they've grown up in an environment where their voices weren't encouraged. The lack of open communication can leave children feeling pressured or emotionally neglected. While rules and boundaries are important, relying solely on this method can lead to emotional distance between parent and child.

Permissive Style: On the opposite end of the spectrum is the permissive parenting style, which emphasizes emotional warmth and support but lacks structure and discipline. Permissive parents are nurturing and affectionate, and they often have close, friendly relationships with their children. However, the downside is that without clear boundaries or expectations, children may struggle to develop self-discipline or understand the importance of limits.

Children raised in permissive households may feel loved and valued, but they might also have difficulty dealing with authority or managing their own behavior. The challenge for permissive parents is finding a way to offer the same emotional support while also setting necessary boundaries to guide their children's growth.

Uninvolved Style: The uninvolved or neglectful parenting style is characterized by a lack of both discipline and emotional involvement. Parents using this approach are often disengaged from their children's lives, providing little guidance, support, or attention. While this style may encourage independence, it often leaves children feeling neglected or abandoned.

Children raised in uninvolved households may struggle with attachment issues, low self-esteem, and difficulties forming relationships. While it's important to give children space to grow and make their own decisions, a lack of parental involvement can lead to long-term emotional and developmental problems.

Achieving a Balanced Parenting Style

Achieving a balanced parenting style involves integrating the strengths of the four main styles to create a nurturing, supportive, and structured environment for your child. The balanced approach adapts to the needs of both the child and the situation, providing structure and discipline when necessary while also offering emotional support and understanding.

For example, you can adopt the authoritative approach when setting rules, ensuring your child understands the reasons behind them and feels heard. At the same time, there may be moments when the authoritarian style is needed—perhaps in situations where safety is a concern, and immediate compliance is crucial. However, even in these moments, it's important to return to a place of emotional connection once the situation is resolved.

Similarly, the permissive style can be useful when children need extra emotional support or encouragement. Showing affection and giving your child space to express their feelings helps build a sense of security. However, it's crucial to balance this with clear expectations and boundaries to ensure they still develop self-discipline.

Lastly, while the uninvolved style is generally considered harmful, there may be instances where it's appropriate to give children independence. Allowing them space to solve their own problems or make decisions without constant oversight can help foster resilience and self-reliance. However, this should always be balanced with the emotional support they need to feel secure and valued.

By blending these styles, you can create a parenting approach that is flexible, responsive, and attuned to your child's individual needs. You and your partner should work together to understand each other's natural parenting tendencies, discuss which approaches work best in different situations, and adapt accordingly. A balanced style ensures that children benefit from both the discipline needed to guide their behavior and the emotional support necessary for their development.

Align Parenting Styles

Start by identifying areas where your styles overlap—perhaps you both value clear communication or emphasize the importance of education. Then, focus on the differences. Where do you tend to disagree, and why? Discuss how to address these differences in a way that presents a united front for your children. This might involve compromise, setting boundaries for when flexibility is allowed, or agreeing on specific areas where one parent may take the lead. The goal is to align on the core principles of parenting, so your children feel the consistency and support of both parents.

STYLES OVERLAP	STYLES OVERLAP

COMPROMISES

Family Bonding Activities

Family bonding activities are a wonderful way to strengthen relationships and create lasting memories. In this exercise, you and your partner will plan regular activities that bring the whole family together, focusing on creating shared experiences that foster connection, communication, and fun.

These activities can be simple and routine, such as family dinners, game nights, or movie marathons, or they can involve more special occasions like day trips, camping, or participating in community events. The key is to choose activities that everyone enjoys and that encourage togetherness. Take turns planning different activities to ensure that all family members' interests are considered. After each activity, reflect on what worked well and what could be adjusted to make future bonding moments even more meaningful.

FAMILY ACTIVITIES	PLANNED	DONE!

Children's Needs Discussion

In this exercise, the goal is to have an open and honest discussion about the individual needs of your children and how you can best meet them as a team.

Start by identifying each child's strengths, areas of growth, and current challenges. Discuss how each of you has been addressing these needs and what adjustments might improve your child's experience. Consider topics like emotional support, academic challenges, social interactions, and physical health. Are there areas where your child needs more guidance, or could benefit from more independence?

By openly discussing your children's needs, you can ensure that both parents are on the same page and working together to provide the best possible environment for your child's development. This discussion also helps foster a more proactive approach to parenting, where each partner is more attuned to the needs of the children and how they can contribute to meeting them.

STRENGHTS	AREAS OF GROWTH

EMOTIONAL SUPPORT

ACADEMIC CHALLENGES

SOCIAL INTERACTIONS

PHYSICAL HEALTH

STRENGHTS	AREAS OF GROWTH

EMOTIONAL SUPPORT

ACADEMIC CHALLENGES

SOCIAL INTERACTIONS

PHYSICAL HEALTH

Extra

Healing from Past Trauma

It's essential to address the profound impact trauma can have on relationships, both consciously and unconsciously. Traumatic experiences, especially those rooted in childhood, often shape how we react to our partner, influence our behaviors, and even dictate our ability to connect emotionally. Many times, what seems like a disproportionate reaction to a partner's comment or action is deeply rooted in unresolved trauma from earlier in life.

Trauma can manifest in a variety of ways in a relationship. Some people might withdraw emotionally, afraid of becoming too vulnerable, while others might be hyper-vigilant, always expecting things to go wrong. In either case, these behaviors stem from the protective mechanisms we develop as children to cope with emotional pain. Unfortunately, those coping mechanisms, which may have been necessary for survival, can hinder the development of a healthy, loving relationship in adulthood.

For example, someone who grew up in a household where affection was rare or inconsistent might struggle with showing or receiving love. They may unconsciously put up walls to protect themselves from the fear of abandonment. Similarly, a person who experienced criticism or emotional neglect as a child might become defensive or overly critical in their relationship, projecting their unresolved pain onto their partner. The reality is that unresolved trauma can keep us stuck in emotional patterns that feel impossible to break, leading to repeated cycles of conflict, disconnection, and misunderstanding in our romantic relationships.

I can relate personally to this experience. Growing up in an emotionally unstable family, I witnessed little affection and a lot of unresolved tension between my parents. The tension was always palpable, with frequent arguments, criticism, and emotional distance. As a result, when I grew older, I found it difficult to show affection in relationships and became extremely cautious about committing to a serious partnership. Getting into a healthy, balanced relationship felt like an overwhelming task, and I often found myself trapped in old emotional patterns that mirrored the environment I had grown up in. I had to work hard on myself, recognizing the trauma I carried and the effects it had on my ability to connect with others. It was a journey of inner healing, understanding my childhood wounds, and consciously choosing to approach relationships differently.

Healing trauma in a relationship is a journey that often begins individually. While mutual support is a critical aspect of healing together as a couple, the initial phase often requires personal reflection and work. This is because trauma affects each partner differently, and it's crucial to acknowledge and address your own emotional wounds before fully engaging in the process of healing as a couple. Doing so not only strengthens your relationship but also helps prevent you from unconsciously reenacting past traumas with your partner.

One powerful step in trauma healing is inner child work. Often, the parts of ourselves that have been hurt the most—those early wounds from childhood—continue to affect us in adult relationships. When we take the time to reconnect with the child within, to offer the understanding and love that might have been missing in our early years, we begin to heal from the inside out. This healing can lead to profound changes in how we show up for our partners, allowing us to form healthier, more secure attachments.

However, the process of healing trauma, especially childhood trauma, can be complex and may require dedicated focus over time. It's often a journey that unfolds in layers, and the depth of this work sometimes goes beyond the scope of relationship counseling alone. For this reason, I strongly encourage you to explore more deeply the concept of inner child healing.

 "**Your Inner Child Healing Journey**" offers tools, exercises, and insights to help you connect with your inner child, heal from the past, and create the emotional freedom necessary to thrive both as an individual and in your relationships. By healing individually, you and your partner will be better equipped to support one another in your shared healing journey, fostering a relationship built on mutual understanding, compassion, and emotional resilience.

As you begin this journey together, you can start by identifying and reflecting on patterns in your relationship without diving straight into the deeper work of inner child healing. Pay attention to recurring themes: Do certain conflicts arise repeatedly? Is there a pattern of withdrawal, avoidance, or overly emotional reactions?

Use the following reflections to guide your awareness:

- *What emotions or reactions come up in heated moments?* Ask yourself if the intensity of your response matches the current situation or if it feels familiar to something from the past.

- *How do you typically handle emotional stress in the relationship?* Are there moments when you shut down or, conversely, feel overwhelmed with the need to be heard?

- *Do you notice any repeated fears or insecurities surfacing during arguments?* Reflect on whether these feelings might be related to experiences from childhood, such as fear of abandonment or rejection.

- *Can you identify areas where you tend to project your past onto your partner?* This could involve expecting your partner to respond in the same negative way a caregiver did, even when they have shown otherwise.

By beginning with these questions, you can gradually bring awareness to emotional triggers and develop a sense of how unresolved trauma might be impacting your relationship. As you reflect, discuss these insights with your partner, making space for mutual understanding. Approach the journey of healing with empathy and patience, recognizing that this work can be challenging but ultimately rewarding.

In the meantime, as you reflect on your relationship and any emotional wounds that may surface, remember that healing is a process—one that requires patience, compassion, and, most importantly, self-love. Supporting each other through trauma can lead to deeper levels of connection, but the foundation for that healing starts with you.

7-Week
Guided Conversations

Guided conversations provide a powerful way to strengthen the bond between partners, allowing you to explore important aspects of your relationship in a structured and meaningful way. By setting aside dedicated time each week for these conversations, you create an opportunity to connect deeply, address potential issues, and work on areas of growth. Throughout this book, we have touched on many topics that are essential to the health of your relationship, and these guided conversations are designed to help you explore them together.

The guided conversations included here are based on the content of the book, offering you and your partner a chance to dive into specific subjects and practice the tools you've learned. These conversations aren't just about solving problems—they are about creating a space for open, honest dialogue that strengthens trust and fosters understanding.

By engaging in these weekly guided conversations, you move beyond casual chats and into meaningful discussions that build a deeper connection. Each week, choose a topic from the guided conversations provided, set aside uninterrupted time, and approach the discussion with openness and curiosity.

Week 1: Communication Basics

- **Goal:** Improve basic communication skills and understand each other's communication style.
- **Opening Prompt:** "How do you feel about our communication right now? What do you think we do well, and what could we improve?"
- **Listening Exercise:** Each partner takes turns explaining how they like to communicate—do you prefer direct or indirect communication? Are you more verbal or non-verbal in expressing feelings?
- **Reflective Question:** "When was the last time we misunderstood each other? How could we have communicated more clearly?"
- **Closing Question:** "What is one specific way we can improve our communication this week?"

Week 2: Trust Building

- **Goal:** Build and strengthen trust through honesty, transparency, and mutual respect.
- **Opening Prompt:** "How do you currently feel about the level of trust in our relationship?"
- **Honesty Exercise:** Share a recent moment where you either built or broke trust, and explain how it made you feel.
- **Reflective Question:** "What actions make you feel more secure in our relationship? What actions cause you to feel uncertain?"
- **Closing Question:** "What's one small step we can take this week to deepen trust between us?"

Week 3: Emotional Intimacy

- **Goal:** Deepen emotional connection and understand each other's emotional needs.
- **Opening Prompt:** "How emotionally connected do you feel with me right now? What makes you feel close to me?"
- **Sharing Exercise:** Each partner shares a personal experience or feeling that they've been holding back. Reflect on why it was difficult to share and how it feels now.
- **Reflective Question:** "What could I do to make you feel more emotionally supported and connected?"
- **Closing Question:** "What's one way we can work together to strengthen our emotional bond this week?"

Week 4: Physical Connection

- **Goal:** Explore the role of physical connection and improve intimacy.
- **Opening Prompt:** "How do you feel about our physical connection? Is there anything you'd like more of, or something we should adjust?"
- **Intimacy Reflection:** Share what physical touch or intimacy means to you—whether it's holding hands, cuddling, or more sexual intimacy—and how it contributes to your emotional closeness.
- **Reflective Question:** "When do you feel most physically connected with me? When do you feel least connected?"
- **Closing Question:** "What's one way we can prioritize physical connection this week?"

Week 5: Conflict Resolution

- **Goal:** Learn how to approach conflicts in a constructive, collaborative way.
- **Opening Prompt:** "How do you think we currently handle conflicts? What do we do well, and where can we improve?"
- **Conflict Analysis:** Think back to a recent disagreement. What was the issue, and how did you each handle it? How could the resolution process have been improved?
- **Reflective Question:** "How can we create a safe space for each other during conflicts, without shutting down or getting defensive?"
- **Closing Question**: "What's one strategy we can implement this week to resolve conflicts more effectively?" _____

Week 6: Balancing Responsibilities

- **Goal:** Create a shared understanding and balance of responsibilities in the relationship.
- **Opening Prompt:** "Do you feel that our household responsibilities are fairly divided? If not, how can we make it more balanced?"
- **Responsibility Discussion:** Each partner lists the responsibilities they handle regularly and discusses how they feel about the balance.
- **Reflective Question:** "What responsibilities are you most comfortable with, and which ones would you like more support in managing?"
- **Closing Question:** "What's one small adjustment we can make this week to better balance our responsibilities?"

Week 7: Long-Term Vision

- **Goal:** Align your long-term goals as a couple and create a vision for your future together.
- **Opening Prompt:** "What do you envision for us in the next 5, 10, or 20 years? What are some of the major goals you want us to achieve?"
- **Vision Sharing:** Each partner shares their dreams, hopes, and plans for the future—whether it's about career, family, travel, or personal growth.
- **Reflective Question:** "How can we better support each other's long-term goals while also building a shared future?"
- **Closing Question:** "What's one long-term goal we can start working towards together this week?"

Extra Week: Parenting Challenges

- **Goal:** Address parenting challenges and align on strategies for raising children together.
- **Opening Prompt:** "How do you feel about our current approach to parenting? Are there any areas where you feel we're not aligned?"
- **Parenting Style Discussion:** Share your parenting styles—how do you see your role as a parent, and what values are most important to you when raising your children?
- **Reflective Question**: "What parenting challenges have been the most difficult for us to navigate, and how can we work together to overcome them?"
- **Closing Question**: "What's one parenting challenge we can tackle together this week?"

Create Your Guided Conversations

The fun part about guided conversations is that you and your partner can take ownership of the process by creating your own conversation scripts on any topic that feels important or challenging in your relationship. These weekly scripts give you a framework for discussing sensitive or recurring issues in a constructive and supportive manner, but you can adapt the approach to address any topic you wish to explore together.

The key is to follow the same logic used in the prompts you've seen: start with an opening question that sets the stage for open communication, create space for reflection, and finish with a clear, actionable step. This structure ensures that you're not just talking about your feelings or frustrations, but that you're working towards a solution that strengthens your connection.

When creating your own guided conversations, it helps to start with a specific topic or challenge. Maybe it's about navigating work-life balance, dealing with extended family dynamics, or planning for a major life change like a move or new career opportunity. Choose an area where you've noticed tension or where you feel like you're not fully on the same page. Then, follow a similar approach:

1. **Start with an opening question:** Think of a question that invites your partner into the conversation without making them feel defensive. For example, instead of saying, "Why don't you ever help around the house?" you could ask, "How do you feel about how we currently manage our household responsibilities?"

2. **Encourage reflection and sharing:** Give your partner the space to share their perspective, and listen actively. You can include prompts that ask them to reflect on recent experiences or explore how they feel about the topic. This is a good time to practice "I" statements, where you share your own thoughts without blaming or accusing your partner.

3. **Close with an action or solution:** The goal of these conversations is not just to express frustrations or complaints but to come up with ways to move forward. After discussing the issue, work together to identify one small, tangible step that can improve the situation. This could be as simple as agreeing to check in more often during the day or planning a regular time to reconnect each week.

And don't forget, if the conversation starts to get heated or emotions run high, the Time-Out Strategy is always available. Take a short break, do something calming, and return to the conversation when you're both feeling more grounded. Time-outs allow you to come back to the discussion with a clearer mind, which helps keep the dialogue constructive rather than reactive.

Creating your own guided conversations is a valuable skill for maintaining the health of your relationship, and the framework you've learned in this book can be applied to any topic that arises. Whether you're talking about everyday concerns or more significant life decisions, having a roadmap for respectful, meaningful conversations will help you and your partner continue to grow together.

Conclusion

Learning to receive and reciprocate love in all its aspects revolves around progress. As you move from one stage to another, resolve one dispute, and make better decisions, you achieve milestones that gradually form the fundamental threshold upon which your relationship will survive. For instance, taking your love to the next level is not necessarily challenging despite the differences you've encountered.

However, even with these achievements, it is also true that love is not an easy adventure. Still, as you move gradually towards the next goal, you get to say, "Thanks to the hurdles we've overcome together, I think we are in a better place now as partners."

I should also tell you that moments of celebration are not just to celebrate the past. Taking note of the good things and dedicating time to celebrating those things gives you access to spending quality time together. Refreshing your love life with a little party effortlessly opens the door to properly planning and discussing the necessary parts of your relationship that need to be improved.

A rich and productive life together is possible if you both learn to incorporate gratitude and appreciation into your relationship. Gratitude is a feeling that brings positivity, hope, and satisfaction into our lives. You do not necessarily need to have everything in the proper order before you learn the power of gratitude; instead, being grateful allows you to appreciate the instant achievements while you look forward to what is to come.

Take note of the change in your relationship and use this celebration to improve your time together. Things like your first anniversary, a change in your relationship status, the decision to move in together, starting a family, and finding out about your first child can be celebrated occasionally.

Understanding the importance of significant milestones in your relationship is a habit you and your partner must develop over time. Learning to love someone requires more than merely saying it. In reality, adequate effort and concentration allow you to express your love to each other through action. Notably, keeping track of relationship achievements, keeping the dates, and making plans to celebrate those achievements communicate the importance of your partner's presence without saying a word.

Moments worth celebrating are uncovered when you practice gratitude, and you can only find reasons to be grateful if you take a moment to reflect on your relationship, the hard times, the good times and the times when your differences or disagreements seem so prominent that you think they can tear you apart.

Generally, there are things to appreciate and celebrate in life or relationships; however, taking a reflective walk into the past is how you identify those things. And as you look into the past, you will find the things worthy of a little party, a bottle of your favorite wine or revisiting some of your favorite places.

Deepn Your Connection Even More!

Inside this book, you've already discovered powerful techniques to enhance your relationship. But what if you could go even further? Whether you're looking to create unforgettable memories, have deeper conversations, or heal from past hurts, we've got you covered. Introducing 4 EXCLUSIVE BONUSES that will transform your relationship:

Creative Date Night Ideas for Intimacy

Never run out of ways to connect on a deeper level. These ideas are designed to bring you closer, spark fun, and keep the romance alive.

Forgiveness Meditation

Heal old wounds and move forward together with this guided meditation, created to help you let go and embrace a future filled with love and understanding.

Relationship Check-In Journal

Stay connected with this simple, yet powerful tool that encourages weekly reflections, helping you both stay on the same page and grow together.

Connection-Building Conversation Starters

Dive into meaningful conversations that uncover new layers of your relationship, making every discussion a chance to bond more deeply.

Simply scan this QR-Code to download these incredible resources and begin experiencing the benefits right away.

Your relationship deserves the best, and these tools are here to help you achieve it.

BOOKSQUARE
PUBLISHING

Your Inner Child Healing Journey

How to Uncover and Heal Deep-Rooted Trauma. A CBT Workbook and Journal to Face Abandonament, Neglet and Abuse, Improve Self-Esteem & Regain Emotional Freedom

Samantha Jones

The Somatic Toolbox

Guidebook, Exercises & Deep-Dive Workbook Activities with a 28-Day Program to Increase Self-Awareness, Heal Trauma, Release Pent-up Emotions & Stress in Just 15 Minutes a Day

Ashely Wellspring

Self Love Workbook

A Guided Journey with Life-Changing Activities & Self-Care Rituals to Truly Fall in Love with Yourself. Heal Emotional Wounds, Recognize Your Worth & Embrace Your Uniqueness

Frida Elowen

Made in the USA
Coppell, TX
17 February 2025

46049701R00070